MAXIMUM
IMPACT
POTENTIAL

MAXIMUM IMPACT POTENTIAL

HOW TO OWN YOUR VALUE, BECOME A WEALTH CIRCULATOR, AND UPLIFT MILLIONS

ALOK APPADURAI

WORLDCHANGERS
MEDIA

DEDICATION

This book is dedicated to ...

My son, Sequoia: the day you were born was singularly the greatest day of my life. Thank you for choosing me to be your daddy. I love you with my full heart.

My late mother, Carol: you taught me how to be a good human being, and showed me what love is all about. Not a day goes by that I don't think about you. I love you, Mom.

My dad, Arjun: you've been by my side as my best friend and confidant through all my ups and downs. You've cheered me on and believed in me. You've been a rock in my life. Thank you for being the best father you could be, and providing the best life for me you could. I love you, Dad.

For Jason Cohen, my oldest friend in the world, who passed far too early: I smile thinking about all the late-night debates this book might have instigated between us. Row-Sham-Bow my dearest friend..

To all of those who backed me when I first conceived this book project back in 2016: Top Backer John Wilson, Bozoma

Saint John, Kathleen Kulenych, Lynn Kaufman, Raphael Emmanuel Fuchs, Stacey Cavin, Mindy Sperlin Mercado, Riisa Mandel, Deb Oliver, and Bonnie Gradillas. Thank you for your faith in me. I'm so proud to finally deliver on my promise to you!

And finally, to all those who have made an impact in my life and helped to shape me into the man I have become: the entirety of this book could not contain all of your names, but know that you are recognized and loved.

PRAISE

"In a world where people are so hungry to make an impact but so lost as to their own potential, Alok gently opens the door for people to see their own light. *Maximum Impact Potential* is a rare find: a book that stirs you, encourages you, and rattles you to step up to the life you were meant to live. Read it in one sitting because life is short and your potential is waiting!"

— **Suzanne Evans,** *New York Times* **best-selling author and founder of Driven, Inc.**

CONTENTS

PART III | UPLIFT MILLIONS

INTRODUCTION

I'LL NEVER FORGET the day my dad took me to Pier 67 on Manhattan's West Side and shared his experience of coming to America.

Looking out over the dark, choppy water of the Hudson River, I tried to picture what it must have been like for him—a young intellectual, recently accepted to Brandeis University, setting foot on those teeming docks after a days-long journey with nothing but his suitcases and a dream.

My father was born in Mumbai to a large Brahmin family. As the youngest of all, he was steeped in the Indian culture of the time. His brothers would go on to choose more traditional paths: One was a railway engineer. Another was in the Army. But my dad wanted something different. He had a prodigious mind and a vast curiosity about both past and present cultures and social orders. Engineering, while a worthy career, was simply not going to cut it for him.

And so, in 1966, while in college in India, he tracked down brochures from American universities and began applying for admission. After being accepted at Brandeis, he flew to London, where two of his brothers were based, and then boarded a boat for New York. I can't imagine the level of courage and conviction it must have taken for him to relocate, alone, to a country across the world.

My dad's career is long and accomplished, so I'll give you the short version: He went on to teach at top-tier universities like the University of Pennsylvania, Stanford, Princeton, Yale, NYU, and the University of Chicago. His theories and published works on globalization, financial crises, ethnic violence, and numerous other commentaries on our social fabric have reshaped the field of anthropology more than once. He has spoken at the UN, UNESCO, World Economic Forum, and numerous other international forums in more countries than I can count. To say I am super proud to be his son would be an enormous understatement.

But that's not why I'm sharing his story.

You see, my parents were my first examples of what it means to pursue your Maximum Impact Potential—the biggest, farthest-reaching impact you can create in a single lifetime. My father is a genius. He could have succeeded in any profession he chose. He could have been a lawyer, an engineer, or a politician (any of which may have been easier for his parents, siblings, and peers to embrace than anthropology). Instead, he has used his limitless intellectual curiosity, research, writing, teaching, and speaking to reshape the way we think about globalization and human society—what it means, how it functions, and where we go from here. He had a dream to change something about how we see the world, and he followed it, even when it would have been easier to do otherwise.

My father, Dr. Arjun Appadurai, chose the path of impact. And for that, he is my hero.

IT'S TIME TO MAKE WAVES

My dad's work inspired me to see the world differently. We aren't a collection of separate individuals who occasionally bump into each other as we make our way through life; we are like molecules of water, part of the great ocean of humanity. When we act, we create waves that ripple far beyond the space we occupy. And, because we are so interconnected, we can't separate from the whole without losing something fundamental about ourselves.

When I first conceived the idea of Maximum Impact Potential—what it means, how it happens, how our choices increase or diminish it—I thought immediately of my dad, and the two biggest lessons I learned from him. I want to share them with you, because they are vital to helping you get the most out of this book.

First, stay curious. If you want to keep expanding the ripple of your presence, your voice, your work in the world, you will need to commit to learning and growth. When your work is informed by an understanding of what people and groups actually need (as opposed to what you think they should want), you will create amazing magnetism in your impact-driven work.

Second, remember that courage, resourcefulness, adaptability, and a willingness to try—even when the odds seem stacked against you—are indispensable when you are committed to impact. As you'll see in this book, the ways in which we have traditionally framed the impact space are both obsolete and counterproductive.

A new model of impact is emerging, and you are being called forward to embody it. In pursuit of your Maximum Impact Potential, you may need to let go of old ideas that no longer serve you, your cause, and your community—especially when it comes to the what, why, and how of impact.

You may need to re-frame ideas and strategies you took for granted. Be willing to become something more than you are today—something more than you can currently imagine—in pursuit of the global change you envision.

Throughout human history, it has been the bolt-loose non-conformers—the idealists, the visionaries, and the thought leaders who serve a purpose greater than themselves—who have always led the charge toward meaningful change. My father knows this from his study of globalization and human society. He passed this knowledge to me, and I have lived it over my more than two decades as an entrepreneur and visionary CEO in the social impact space.

Doing this work is not for the faint of heart—but the rewards, in every area, are virtually unlimited, especially in today's knowledge economy.

If you are committed to creating positive impact in the world—if you are committed to making waves in your industry, your community, or around the planet—you are in the right place.

In this book, I will show you how to own your value, harness the velocity of capital in your business, and create an Impact Empire that will serve the planet in ways beyond what you can possibly imagine at this moment.

I sometimes wonder if my dad imagined, standing there on Pier 67 with only his suitcases and a dream, what he would achieve in the course of his lifetime.

You are standing in a similar place—on the precipice of a new way of working, living, and creating impact on this planet. Your choices in this moment will determine the trajectory of everything that is to come.

Are you ready to take the leap?

PART I

OWN YOUR VALUE

1 | WAKE UP

WHEN I WALKED INTO my parents' apartment at 2:00 a.m. on October 4, 2009, my father was sitting alone on the couch wearing an expression that can only be described as "shell shock." Somewhere off to my left, I could hear my uncle speaking in loud, firm tones to my mother.

I'd been called to my parents' home numerous times over the previous several years, as my mother's journey through cancer intensified and my father's warrior heart became more and more exhausted. But I knew tonight was different. The moment I saw my dad, the entire scene shifted into movie-style slow motion. I don't remember if we spoke, but I know what I was thinking. *It's okay, Dad. It's my turn to step up now.*

I moved through the living room and into the dark hallway beyond. As I passed the bathroom, I saw my uncle's hulking, shirtless back. He was holding my mother up on the toilet, sweat oozing from every pore as he barked at her. "Come on, Carol. Just take a shit already!"

I didn't stop. I just kept walking down the hall to my father's office. Methodically, I undid my tie, stripped off my suit jacket, and rolled up my sleeves in preparation for the battle to come.

I walked into the bathroom and laid my hands on Uncle Jim's drenched shoulders, nodding at him to step aside. It was my turn now. He collapsed into the tub—the only free space in my parents' typically-tight New York City bathroom—gasping for air as he barked the latest medical updates at me.

My mother was constipated and in horrendous pain. The shaved bit of scalp around her chemo port was white and waxy. I bent towards her and slipped my hands under her armpits, feeling the fragility of her body.

"Mom," I whispered. "I'm here. It's me, Alok. Your son." Her body draped itself over my arms in full release and trust.

At some point, a mug of liquid laxative made its way into my hands. "Mom, I need you to drink this." Weakly, her mouth opened to obey my request and I watched her lips move towards the straw. Such a small thing, to take a drink, something that so many of us take for granted—and yet, I could tell it took every drop of will and energy she had to suck the contents of that mug through the straw. In the background, my uncle chattered on, processing in his own way the awfulness of his sister's predicament.

Then, Uncle Jim shouted, "Alok, she's biting her tongue! Jam a toothbrush in her mouth! Arjun, call 9-1-1!"

As I fumbled for a toothbrush, I watched my mother's lower jaw sink back so that her top teeth hung over the lower row ... and I knew. But I shoved the toothbrush in there anyway, a hopeful but futile attempt to avoid the truth.

I waited to feel the rise of her chest, hear the rattle of her breath. But there was nothing.

"Uncle Jim," I said firmly. "She's gone."

My uncle wailed. It sounded like he was screaming from a place in his soul he had never visited before.

I couldn't make a sound.

I dead-lifted my mother off of the toilet, turned her body around, and slid my arms around her from behind. Walking backward, I carried her down the hall to her office and laid with her on the futon, holding her in an embrace that tried to apologize for all the years I withheld my hugs from her.

My dad handed me the phone. The 9-1-1 operator's voice was a calm, methodical drone. "Put your pointer and middle fingers together one inch to the left of her throat, just below the chin. Do you feel a pulse?" I surely had never been taught how to hunt for a heartbeat.

"No," I replied, with the same eerie calm. "There's no pulse."

An eternity later, the paramedics arrived. The first thing they asked was, "Do you have a Do Not Resuscitate form?"

Not once, in all the months of her dying, did one person from my mother's care team suggest that we create a DNR. The lead paramedic put an apologetic hand on my shoulder and said, "I'm so sorry, sir, but you'll have to exit the room as we try to bring your mother back to life."

My mother was dead. She was gone. After her fifteen-year battle with cancer, she should be allowed, at last, to be at peace! Now, because we were missing a single piece of paper, she would be robbed of the protocols and traditions she had learned in my father's native India and brought into our family. A crime of the spirit was about to occur—and there was nothing I could do about it.

As I unclasped my hands from her body and retreated to the open doorway, I swore to my mother I would not leave her. I watched as the paramedics moved her lifeless body down onto the wood floor and began to shock her with their electrical paddles—in short, doing everything they were required, by law, to do to make her heart beat again in the absence of a DNR. Every shock through her convulsing body sent shivers of anger and sadness coursing through mine.

To my horror, they manufactured a pulse. They wheeled in a gurney, strapped my mother's artificially-living body to it, and started the mad dash to the elevators.

That early morning ride through the empty streets of Manhattan, illuminated by the ambulance's flashing red lights and the fizzling streetlamps, was surreal. I was alone with the crew and my swirling thoughts; my father was right behind in a taxi.

By the time we got to the ER, my dad had gotten in touch with someone from the NYU Cancer team and informed them of our lack of a DNR form. Their advice was that we should tell the attending doctor, "Do not escalate"—meaning, the doctor should do absolutely nothing to attempt to improve or sustain my mother's heartbeat.

Maybe it was selfish that we let her go so easily. Maybe neither me nor my father could bear the thought of her being kept alive in that state. Or maybe I just couldn't bear having my mother die a second time.

Upon hearing our wishes, the doctor asked, "You know what that means, right?"

We did. It was what should have been allowed to happen ten blocks from there, in the living room of my parents' eleventh-floor apartment.

Once the intake process was over, Dad and I went outside for some air. The sun was just beginning to rise, turning everything golden. We didn't speak.

Within five minutes, the doctor found us and broke the news.

My mother had died. Again.

***

My mother, Carol A. Breckenridge, modeled a compassionate dedication to service in her lifetime that touched thousands of lives. But it wasn't until her death that I fully internalized the lessons on offer from her life.

The crazy thing was, I almost failed to show up for her that final night. I'd been out drinking at a Midtown loft with friends, celebrating a wedding between two people I loved. As we streamed out of the venue at 1:00 a.m., chattering excitedly about which bar to migrate to next, my phone buzzed with a text from my father.

I could really use your help tonight, it read.

It wasn't unusual for me to get messages like this. Sometimes, I rose to the occasion. Other times, for my own sanity, I declined.

With love-and-wine-stoked laughter swirling around me, my mind went into calculation mode. Yes, Mom was in bad shape, but my dad wasn't alone. Uncle Jim—not a well man himself—had ventured down from Upstate New

York to be with his sister. Plus, I'd been drinking, so I wasn't exactly in the best shape to be a helper.

To avoid the guilt of the decision, I decided on a compromise: rather than head to the next bar with the wedding entourage, I would grab a cab and head back to my place in Brooklyn.

As the cab sped south along the West Side Highway, something gnawed at my gut. Was it God? Fate? Maybe it was just guilt—but whatever it was, I knew that if I went back to Brooklyn that night I would regret it for the rest of my life.

"Exit here," I told the cabbie abruptly. "110 Bleecker Street, please."

"Your call, kid," the cabbie grumbled, swerving onto the exit ramp.

That night was one of the hardest of my life. But I wouldn't have missed it for the world.

At my mother's memorial service, I gave the opening address to a standing-room-only crowd of over 250 people who had showed up to celebrate her contribution to humanity. Before I began, I said to the audience "I'd like every woman whose life has been impacted by my mom to please stand up."

Slowly, one by one, an ocean of powerhouse women began to rise to their feet in silent acknowledgment of the impact my mother had had on their lives.

"Look around," I said, as much to myself as to the crowd.

"You are the living legacy of my mother, Carol." Right in front of my eyes was the ripple effect we each can have when we decide to uplift others.

Everyone in the room had goosebumps. We were seeing the legacy of a life dedicated to *impact.*

My mother was a lifelong feminist, educator, and mentor. Even when she could barely muster the energy to eat and drink, or was recovering from a major procedure, she would spend hours on the phone, advising women about the finer points of their dissertations and how they could pursue their dreams. My father would often tell me, "Oh, she was helping so-and-so with her proposal from the chemo chair today." Her drive to compassionately give of herself—even to those whose work she would never see come to fruition—was incredible.

Even when she knew her time was running out, she wanted to be there for others. My friend, Scott, flew in from Chicago with his fiancée, Aleks, during that last year, because he wanted my mom to meet Aleks before she passed. We all sat in our living room together. They showed my mom the ring and chatted about plans for the wedding.

"Can I come?" my mom asked.

"Of course," Scott said, surprised.

My mom took out her calendar and asked for the dates again—even though we all knew she wouldn't live long enough for her to attend. It didn't matter; the statement she was making was, "I will do everything in my power to be there for you." She knew that the impact created by deep human connection lasts long after we are gone.

DRIVEN BY IMPACT

Right now, as you read these words, you are at a crossroads. You can choose to continue on with life as usual—or you can decide to live a life that changes the world for the better, and harness an energy that I call your Maximum Impact Potential.

Impact is not an accident. It's not a superpower granted to only a chosen few. It's a *decision*—one that you can make in every moment, every day, for the rest of your allotted time here on Earth.

Even before my mother's passing, I had been on the path to making a difference. I'd had several "lightning bolt" moments in my childhood (which I'll share with you shortly) that kindled a desire to create a meaningful life. I went on to become a teacher in a private school in New York, contributing to the development of young minds with all the fervor of someone born into a family of educators. But while I was doing good work, I wasn't even close to reaching my Maximum Impact Potential—and I knew it.

Once my mother was gone, however, I fully committed—to myself, to her, and the higher power of my understanding—to making the biggest difference in this world possible. I made a powerful decision to create my way out of the jumbled human soup of emotions, behaviors, inspirations, desires, guilts, and gratitudes, and design a purpose-driven life. To let my mission be bigger than my fear. To live, work, and dream in a way that uplifts millions.

Maybe you feel that same drive. You *know* you're here for a reason, and you're willing to do, be, and create whatever it takes to fulfill that purpose.

Or, maybe you're struggling to create a business that actually moves the needle in the direction of the change you want to make. Maybe you've found your impact space, but you haven't figured out how to start busting through like a meteorite instead of feeling like a pebble in a pond. Or maybe you're already doing big things in your industry, but you're burned out and struggling to remember *why* you started this thing in the first place.

If any of these sound like you, you're in the right place.

I believe that *all of us* are born with a heart of service. We want to help others. We want to be part of something bigger than ourselves. We want to leave the world a better place than we found it, for both current and future generations.

I also believe that every single one of us has the capability to live up to—and into—our Maximum Impact Potential, regardless of where we come from, what we look like, or what challenges life has thrown our way.

I'll speak into these philosophies more deeply later in this book, but for now, know that once you *decide* to become the version of you who is here to make a massive impact, and become willing to do what it takes to walk that path, there is nothing "out there" that can stop you. *Nothing.*

When you follow this path, you'll come face to face with some deep truths. You'll need to look at everything in your life and business in a new light. You'll need to unlearn some of the crazy, limiting shit you've absorbed in your human journey, and relearn new truths that at first will seem even crazier. You'll need to *completely shift* your relationship to money. You'll need to learn how to operate as part of a diverse human ecosystem, not an island in a sea of oppression and competition.

I can't guarantee this will be easy. In fact, it most likely will be the biggest challenge of your life to date. But I promise, it will be worth it.

YOU ARE DESIGNED TO MAKE A DIFFERENCE

As you may have guessed from the title of this book, I'm about to teach you the formula for creating your Maximum Impact Potential.

So ... what is MIP?

If you've been in the entrepreneurial world for a while, you've probably heard the term "Minimum Viable Product," or MVP. This concept is about creating a product or service with the fewest number of features necessary to create the desired result. It's a "shortcut" for developers that lets them get to the heart of their product's usability, function, and intended impact.

Similarly, your Maximum Impact Potential is about creating and leading from a *point of impact* rather than a product or process. It's about using every breath still available to you to uplift others and the planet—and at the same time, shortcut the bullshit that so many of us get tangled in as we strive to make our lives meaningful.

You make choices every day. Small choices. Big choices. Choices that don't feel like choices at all. These accumulated daily decisions have established your current MIP— the projected level of change you will create in the time left to you on this planet.

If that made you think, "Oh, shit," don't worry. MIP isn't fixed. It's a metric that's constantly fluctuating, like a stock ticker in the financial markets. Just as companies can make decisions that set them up for explosive growth in the market (or crash them in a heartbeat), you have the power and ability—today, tomorrow, and every day—to raise your "impact meter" through your choices and actions.

Once you understand this, there's no going back. You will feel the power of your small, daily decisions—as well as your huge, courageous ones—in a new way. You will see each new day as an opportunity to scale your Impact Empire.

We can never get back the life energy we've already spent. But we can make a powerful choice, right now, to live as though every second matters. Because it does.

LIVING LIFE IN REVERSE

There were many unusual things about my childhood, but the one that always stood out to me was the contrast.

My parents weren't poor. They both had PhDs. They were teachers and academics. I went to upscale private schools. And yet, we lived for much of my childhood in West Philadelphia, in a neighborhood where the sounds of gunshots and sirens weren't infrequent. A kid I played basketball with got shot at the deli two blocks away. We weren't personally hungry or scraping to pay the mortgage—but the harsh realities of poverty, alcoholism, and violence were all too immediate for many people around us.

On my trips to see my father's family in India, the contrast was amplified even further. It was hard for me, as a little kid, to reconcile our relative abundance with the level of poverty I saw in Bombay. I didn't understand how things could be so unequal, or so unfair.

I decided that, when I grew up, I was going to have lots and lots of money. And I was going to use it to help people.

Fast forward to 1997. I was nineteen, and had been

accepted to Wesleyan University, where I was studying to become an investment banker. I was definitely on track to make a shit-ton of money—but I had lost my connection to the reasons why I *wanted* that money. My dreams then were about sports cars and gleaming mansions, not feeding the hungry.

That winter, my parents and I went back to India again. While we were there, my dad hired a driver to take us from Delhi to Agra so we could visit the Taj Mahal, one of the wonders of the world.

For those who have never driven in India: it's a life-changing experience.

My parents were in the backseat. I was in the third row, which was rear-facing. As the car sped along, careening around corners and playing chicken with oncoming traffic, I watched all our near-misses unfold behind us in slow motion. We were literally escaping death every hundred yards.

Suddenly, I wasn't alone in the backseat. My eighty-year-old self was sitting next to me.

In my state of heightened awareness, this didn't seem odd at all.

As I hung on to my seat for dear life, Future Alok started to speak. He told me about his career in investment banking, the deals he'd chased, the people he'd hung out with, the cars and mansions and boats he'd bought. He told me how he'd put profits over people, the planet, and even his personal relationships. Sure, he gave millions to charities and helped out his family—he was even considered a "philanthropist"—but now, at the end of his life, he was full of regret.

In that moment, I literally saw his life—*my* life—unfold in front of me. If I continued on the path I'd chosen, I would burn away the next sixty years extracting as much wealth as I could from the world. I would be rich beyond anything I'd ever seen or dreamed about. But I would never be happy. I would never feel fulfilled. And I would leave this world with the gut-gnawing certainty that my life hadn't really *mattered.*

At that moment, I vowed to rewrite that history.

As the car flew along the mountain roads, I promised my eighty-year-old self that I would be the man he hadn't been in life. I would change our story, and treat my time on this planet as the precious gift it was.

My path was clear: do as much good as possible. Do it often. Do it again and again.

When we were finally safe in Delhi again, I fulfilled my promise to my older self, and wrote him a new obituary. In it, I described all the things he had accomplished in life. He provided a billion meals to those in need. He planted a billion trees. He pursued what mattered—not just to him, but to the planet. He still made lots of money, but he used that capital as a vehicle for massive change.

And when he died at the age of eighty-nine, he had *not*

one single regret.

Something magical happened when I wrote that obituary: I stopped fearing death. If I could truly live into my Maximum Impact Potential every day, I would leave this world knowing that I had given my all. It was an inspiring exercise, one I have repeated again and again at various points in my life.

When I got back to university that next semester, I completely rebuilt my major to focus on History, Economics, and Literature so I could better understand the world we live in. I had no idea where this new road would lead me, but I knew I had to find out. I was on a quest to realize my Maximum Impact Potential.

Those moments on the drive to Agra are with me every day. Have I always lived into my MIP? Fuck, no. Have I lost my way for months, even years at a time? You bet. But when I get off track, I always come back around and ask, "Am I living in a way that would make my eighty-year-old self proud?" If the answer isn't a resounding, "Hell yes!" I know something needs to shift.

If you've never written your own obituary, I highly recommend it as an exercise. In fact, dog-ear this page, grab your notebook, and do it now. I promise, it will give you a whole new perspective on what "a life with no regrets" means to you.

HARDWIRED FOR IMPACT

The most natural way for humans to relate to one another—in relationships, social groups, and societies—is through caring and service to others. All of us (with the notable exception of sociopaths) are seeking this kind of connection and appreciation. We feel good when we make others feel good.

Other people have explored in depth the neurological benefits of giving—including increases in dopamine, serotonin, and oxytocin, aka the "happiness trifecta"—so I won't explain the mechanics here. The truth is, uplifting others is a drug of the best variety; once you get hooked, there's no going back. The shift from "me" to "we" taps into ancestral DNA coding that society has done a bang-up job of burying beneath shallow cravings that leave most of us unfulfilled.

I want you to absorb the truth that you, along with every other human on this planet, are designed to make a tremendous difference in the lives of others. You are literally *hardwired* for impact—and when you make impact the focus of your life, there is no limit to the happiness, satisfaction, connection, and joy you can achieve.

Impact occurs the moment you begin to ask yourself, "What is my Maximum Impact Potential?" In that split second, you literally go from living on autopilot to living a purpose-driven lifestyle. That "me to we" shift taps into a timeless and primal power source inside you that is Universal;

it makes achieving your MIP a forgone conclusion.

Realizing my MIP is what gets me out of bed in the morning. It's what inspires me to coach my clients and students to make powerful decisions and step into their own greatness. It's what motivates me to meet challenges head- on, and what keeps me from melting into a stagnant, Netflix-bingeing, beer-drenched puddle on the couch when life feels overwhelming. It was what dragged my ass out of the gutter when I lost everything in 2016 (more on that later), and what inspires me to keep growing and expanding my Impact Empire today, even though traditional thinking would say I've "made it" many times over.

Most of all, living into my MIP means that, if I died tomorrow, I'd know beyond a doubt that my eighty-year-old self would be proud—and that my only regret would be leaving my son, Sequoia, without his dad.

HOW TO USE THIS BOOK

Whether you're already living into your MIP every day, or you're just having that "come-to-Jesus" moment with your own eighty-year-old self, this book is your definitive guide to growing your Impact Empire and changing the world for the better.

It's also a direct challenge to some of the biggest "truths" you've learned as an entrepreneur and human being.

You see, impact requires three things:

1. Decision
2. Vision
3. Leverage

Decision is exactly that: your powerful choice to do what it takes to make a difference in the lives of others and create your personal definition of a meaningful life. It's a power and a privilege you exercise every day, and the key that unlocks every door.

Vision is the "how" of your Maximum Impact Potential. When you create an impact-centric vision, you become an architect of your life, future-planning your path to becoming a part of something bigger than yourself. Without a clear vision for your MIP (or any other aspect of your work), you will always under-perform.

Leverage is what you need to fuel your Decision and Vision and actually make shit happen. It's time, resources, and "people power." But most of all, it's *money*.

Wealth is the secret weapon in your mission to create your Maximum Impact Potential. Align with it, and you will become unstoppable. Fail to mobilize it, and your vision will wither.

Given what I just shared about my conversation with my eighty-year-old self, this truth may shock you. But money itself wasn't the issue in the life path I glimpsed. It was money used and pursued selfishly, though the wrong channels, for the wrong reasons. It was *money absent consciousness.*

By the time you turn the last page of this book, you'll understand how these three ingredients—Decision, Vision, and Leverage—work synergistically to create massive impact, and how you can harness them in your own work to fulfill your Maximum Impact Potential.

So open your mind, toss your excuses out the window, and let's dive in.

2 | IMPACT IS AN INNER GAME

W HEN I WAS in college, I spent a winter break in Chicago with some friends of mine. One night, we ended up at a local bar shooting pool.

A big group of us were there, including my friend's gorgeous older sister, who I'll call "Gigi." Honestly, she left twenty-year-old me a little tongue tied. Not only was she hot, she (and my buddy) came from money. I mean, *lots* of money. You'd know the family name if I dropped it here.

Since there was only one open pool table, we decided to play partners. I was paired with—you guessed it—Gigi. Hoping to impress her, I pulled off a good break, and sank a couple of balls on my first turn.

I tried to look nonchalant, but inside I was screaming *"Yeeeaaaahhhh, dude!"* I felt like I'd just pulled off a coup.

Eyebrows raised, Gigi leaned over and whispered, "Nice job, Gandhi," referencing my father's country of origin.

The proud butterflies in my gut turned to lead. It was like one of those awkward scenes in a rom-com where the lead character says something completely unacceptable, but no one wants to hurt her feelings so they all whistle and look at the ceiling.

I had no idea if Gigi realized how insulting her comment was. Would informing her just make it worse? What the heck should I do? So, I did nothing. Just high-fived her, and got back to the game.

To my surprise (and everyone else's) my second turn went equally well.

"Great job!" Gigi squealed. "Where'd you learn that? In India?"

I don't know why this second round of insensitivity shocked me even more than the first, but it did. I felt frozen. But again, I said nothing.

Walking back to my buddy's place later, I was seething. I thought about all the things I could have said to stop Gigi in her tracks. Shouldn't I have stood up for myself—and people of Indian descent everywhere? I imagined whipping out my verbal machete and chopping her white privilege into devastatingly small, tearful morsels. Then, just as quickly, I imagined what such a response would do to my friendship with her brother, and my reputation in general. Would it really be worth it?

In the end, my musings were too little, too late. I didn't see Gigi again on that trip. In fact, I didn't see her again for a long time.

I shared that story as an example of inherent bias many times over the course of the next several years. From my more "woke" friends, it elicited a gasp of empathetic disgust. Others would reply, "What's the big deal?"

As I got older, I spent a lot of time studying the "greats" of the impact space: Gandhi (of course), Mother Teresa, Nelson Mandela, Martin Luther King, Jr., and other social impact pioneers. These individuals were regarded as superheroes for their ability to uplift millions and change deep-rooted institutional and cultural biases. I started to wonder what made them tick, and how they were able to get up every day and find the energy to keep pushing toward their lofty, seemingly unattainable goals. Were they somehow different than normal people? Were they born with special DNA that made them more driven, more capable, and more worthy to lead movements?

I began to read voraciously about the lives of these super-human figures. But the more I learned, the more I realized one simple truth:

They were just like me.

In fact, the only difference between me and them was that they *consistently made choices in alignment with their values, vision, and desire for impact,* even against great odds and at great personal sacrifice. They were fully available for impact. They didn't just believe they *could* accomplish their goals; they knew they *must*.

And wasn't that exactly what eighty-year-old Alok had been trying to tell me in the car all those years earlier? That if I wanted to live a life of impact, I needed to *make better choices*?

Understanding this instantly shrunk the massive gap between me and my idols. I realized that my Maximum Impact Potential was equal to that of anyone else on the planet. The same seed of greatness already exists in each of us. Each time we choose our "must" over our "maybe," we nurture that greatness into form in our reality.

About a decade after the pool hall incident, I ran into Gigi at a fundraiser for our private high school. I decided to take the high road and pretend I had zero recollection of her comments all those years before. We caught up on the details of our lives—her kids, my work, our parents' health. She seemed a little jittery, but I couldn't put my finger on why.

Then, just as the school headmaster took the podium and our mingling was cut short, Gigi leaned over and whispered, "Last time I saw you, I called you Gandhi. I am so, *so* sorry for that. It was totally out of line."

I was floored. Not only had she remembered, she'd actually *apologized*? I had never imagined that this moment might come to pass. It felt like coming full circle.

My heart swelled with gratitude. I turned to her and smiled.

"I *am* Gandhi," I whispered.

***

I couldn't explain to Gigi, in that moment, the quest her offhand insult had set me on, or the profound realizations that resulted. Leaning into what it meant to "be Gandhi" helped me to realize the enormity of my own potential.

I am Gandhi. You are Gandhi. We are *all* Gandhi.

Now, I'm not saying you have to love everything about Gandhi, or aspire to be like him in any way. He was human, and far from perfect. What I *am* saying is this: *every single one of us* has the same inborn power and potential to change the world.

What separates you, me, or anyone on this planet from the impact superheroes we revere are our *choices*. It doesn't matter if you grew up on the streets of West Philly or Bombay, or in a warm bubble of privilege in London or Zurich or

Dubai. It doesn't matter what you look like, or where you went to school, or where your parents came from. It doesn't matter what degrees you hold, or even who you know. What matters is that, when the time comes, you choose to live in alignment with the change you want to be in the world.

I find that most people who dream of creating massive impact feel the way I once did: that true "world-changers" are somehow different from the rest of us. Our cultural narratives around impact-makers reflect this sense of them being "the chosen ones." But none of the people we revere were born special. They weren't inherently more qualified than you, or me, or their high school classmates when they started their impact journeys. They were simply willing to do three things: live by their vision, learn what they didn't know, and make powerful decisions.

All of us are constantly exposed to cultural narratives about how we are supposed to live and what it means when we go big with our mission—why it's not okay, why it isn't safe, what people will say about us when we break out of the box. We also have plenty of "evidence" to prove that what we have been told is correct. Some of that evidence is violent and terrifying—particularly for people of color, indigenous people, and LGBTQIA people.

And yet, there are still those who are willing to defy those odds in the name of the change they want to create in the world. Most of the people I admire as leaders became that way *in spite of* what was "acceptable" for them to do and become.

Now, these ideas may rub some the wrong way. Some people clutch onto victim-driven narratives, detailing all the ways in which they are being held back. This only robs them of the truth: that they are a powerful creator, equally endowed with Universal wisdom passed down through generations. So, we each need to make a decision: blame others for why we aren't able to create our MIP, or step boldly into our potential to uplift millions.

As my colleague, Aaron Morrison, says, "You either have reasons, or you have results."

Wangari Muta Maathai, founder of the Green Belt Movement and author of several groundbreaking books including *Unbowed: A Memoir*, was the first woman in East and Central Africa to earn a PhD in Philosophy. By the end of her life, she had empowered thousands of people and planted millions of trees. One of my favorite quotes from her is: "You cannot enslave a mind that knows itself. That values itself. That understands itself."

Maathai's story, like those of so many changemakers, has been wrapped in a sort of mysticism. People think, "She must have had something that 'normal' people don't have. She must have had family connections, or a ton of luck, or something special that isn't available to people like me." This simply isn't true. What she had was vision, determination, and a willingness to learn. She trained her mind to know itself, value itself, and understand itself. After that, she simply committed to doing whatever it took to lean into her vision and keep moving toward her MIP.

The gap you are bridging when you step into your own Maximum Impact Potential isn't between you and some elusive, superhuman ideal. It's the gap between who you're being now and *who your vision is asking you to become.*

When you make a powerful choice to take that leap, you also agree to let go of all the false beliefs about yourself and the world that you've been carrying up until this moment. You agree to free your mind from the enslavement of limitation. You agree to destroy your disempowering guru narratives and value yourself at the same level as you value your greatest heroes.

I can't even tell you how many sneaky ways people find to avoid this truth. One of my favorites is when people say, "I can't do what Dr. King/Oprah/Lisa Nichols did. I'm not a natural orator," or, "I have no business talking about inner peace. I'm not as compassionate as Mother Teresa/the Dalai Lama/Mata Amma."

I've got news for you. Every skill that the changemakers you admire possess is *learnable.*

Oration is learnable. Compassion is learnable. Marketing is learnable. Persistence is learnable.

And, most of all, mindset is *learnable.*

WAITING FOR GOD

When I was six years old, I asked God for a million dollars.

At that time, we were living in Palo Alto, California, since my dad had been invited to teach for a year at Stanford University. I kept a shoebox full of money under my bed: coins, singles, a few fives I'd earned doing chores for my dad, and one precious twenty-dollar bill that had come in a birthday card from my Uncle Jim. I liked having money—and I'd also seen what the lack of money could do to a person, a family, a community. Even when you're six, you can't ignore the grim reality of Bombay's slums or West Philadelphia's rough streets.

Then, I remembered the way my Christian grandparents from Upstate New York always said, "God will provide." I didn't really understand how that worked, but I figured it was worth a try.

So, I asked God to provide. I literally prayed for God to deliver a million dollars—and with my whole heart, I believed that it would happen.

Every morning, filled with hope and anticipation, I would sneak out the front door and run to the mailbox to see if God, in fact, had delivered. With each step, I imagined the sensation of opening the mailbox door and watching hundred-dollar bills burst out. I imagined barely being able to carry that huge pile of cash.

And every day, I pawed through phone bills, electric bills, credit card bills, water bills, and the occasional letter addressed to my mom. Then, finally, after weeks of disappointment, I realized the truth: no dollar bills were going to show up for me.

I was heartbroken. I wondered if I'd done something wrong—if God had somehow decided I was unworthy of receiving what I'd prayed for. I felt abandoned by my higher power.

As I got older, I began to see how my relatives were always asking God for things, but the only way those things actually happened was when they took action to create them for themselves. I didn't understand the theory of co-creation with the universe, manifestation, or the Law of Attraction until later—but it was clear to me, even early on, that just asking wasn't enough.

So many impact-conscious entrepreneurs operate this way. They think that if they're "good" enough, or if their mission is worthy enough, that God, Goddess, Source, The Universe, Ganesh, or whoever will just deliver that million-dollar check to their door. When that doesn't happen, they end up feeling exactly like I did: abandoned, rejected, and confused.

And so, in their heads, they start separating impact from income, and momentum from wealth.

Something shifts. They start talking about money as a

problem to be solved, not a solution to be applied. They bash the people who actually *have* money for being greedy, shit-eating world-destroyers. They say, "I don't care about money. It's not important. All I care about is impact."

This mentality is a huge issue for many of the visionaries I work with. They think wealth consciousness and impact consciousness are separate. They think vision and decision are enough.

I've got news for you. A vision for change is like a pipeline. It's a container, intended to flow energy in a direction. But without resources moving through it, it's just ... a pipe dream. A dry well. Empty, hollow, and effectively useless.

Massive change *requires* money.

Every changemaker, visionary, and social impact superhero you venerate understands this truth in their bones. It's widely believed that Mother Teresa moved billions through her organization in her lifetime, although actual numbers are scarce. Martin Luther King, Jr. fundraised extensively for everything from boycotts to marches. (Those fliers didn't print themselves, you know!) And how do you think the Dalai Lama maintains that security detail, flies all around the world, and hosts gigantic events at pricey venues? You guessed it: with cold, hard cashola.

If you want to create real, lasting impact with your work and in your life, you *must* become a conduit for money. Money is the rocket fuel for your mission, and the cushion for your crash landings. And yet, money is almost never part of the "superhero changemaker" narrative. You don't read about how, precisely, Thich Nhat Hanh funded his foundation (and paid its full-time staff). You don't read about the time Mother Teresa spent gathering financial support for her cause or meeting with billionaire donors.

Without the force of money behind him, even Gandhi would have quickly fizzled into obscurity. He would have become just one more disillusioned dude talking a big game about independence and government reform.

The world doesn't need more big ideas. There are plenty of those. The world needs people who can make powerful decisions, take action, and *move money through their ideas*—courageous souls like you who believe in the power of their work to uplift millions.

The bottom line is, every successful visionary has mastered one key skill: the ability to access reserves of capital. Money powers their missions. It's a top priority; it has to be. Why? Because they know that without it, they would have minimal reach. Minimal leverage. Minimal *impact*.

Wealth consciousness has been a taboo topic in the impact space for far too long. That needs to change—and that change starts in this moment, with you.

I truly believe that God (or the Universe, or whoever) didn't deliver that million dollars to six-year-old me because I didn't have a *purpose* for that money. I hadn't conceived a pipeline to funnel that cash into impact. I didn't tell the Universe *why* I should receive at that scale, or what I planned to do with that wealth once it arrived. I just wanted it in this vague, formless kind of way, because I believed it would make things better.

That vagueness is another issue for many impact-seekers. They have a big vision for global unity or happiness or education, but they have never actually considered what it will take to create it.

Your vision comes with a price tag. Likely an eye-poppingly big one. There's a measurable monetary cost to achieving the change you want to see in the world. Whether you're running an impact-driven coaching business, creating a world-changing consumer product, or running a non-profit, you need to know the price of *each and every change* you want to make so you can move money into that funnel.

I'll show you how to price out your vision in Chapter 8 of this book. But for now, all I'm asking is that you take in what you've learned, and ask yourself: "What kind of money flow will actually allow me to achieve my MIP?"

WEALTH CONSCIOUSNESS IS IMPACT CONSCIOUSNESS

When I was eleven, I began selling water purifiers door-to-door with my Uncle Jim in rural Upstate New York. Many might consider this an unappealing job, but Uncle Jim loved it, and he made a great living at it.

"Alok, I help people have clean water to drink," he told me. "I get to make money *and* feel good about what I'm doing."

This was the beginning of a major transformation for me. I could make money *and* make people's lives better? I loved the idea.

Uncle Jim taught me the two most important lessons about business I have ever learned, and they have stayed with me to this day.

The first: "Sell things that make people's lives better."

The second: "Sell the *best versions* of things that make people's lives better."

At the time, reverse osmosis filtration was the gold standard for home water systems and Uncle Jim sold the best dang RO systems on the market. When he knocked on someone's door, he was confident that he really *could* make someone's life better if they purchased a system from him. His "why" was providing safer, cleaner drinking water for his clients. By filling this need in the market, he was making an impact. The more systems he sold, the more money he made, and the more impact he created.

Uncle Jim was my first example of how wealth consciousness and impact consciousness could intersect.

Of course, the two can exist separately. Plenty of people

make a ton of money without professing any interest in making the world a better place. And plenty of people focus on impact without ever moving money at a large scale. (If you've ever worked at a nonprofit, you probably know what an uphill slog that can be.)

But when the two come together?

Big shit starts to happen.

If you are serious about creating your MIP, you must be willing to let go of any reservations you have about being a conduit for money. Lots and lots of money. Money with more zeros than you've ever seen. Money that can change the world.

If you've got lurking money stuff (and who doesn't), I'm not going to ask or expect that you drop it all at once. Maybe you cringed when you read this section, because you have an ingrained belief that rich people are dicks who don't care about the little guy. Maybe you already have tons of money, but the idea of moving more of it *through* you for impact feels risky and unsafe. Maybe you had money, and then lost it—so how could you possibly become a *bigger* conduit to create impact?

It doesn't matter what your money story is. What matters now, in this moment, is that you make a powerful decision to become the version of you who can be a conduit for wealth as well as a nexus for impact. Only then can you start doing the work of healing your money traumas and creating your Maximum Impact Potential.

If you try to live into your MIP without doing the work to become a conduit for wealth, you will always—and I mean *always*—sell yourself short on the impact you are capable of creating. On the other hand, when you combine wealth consciousness and impact consciousness, you are signaling to the Universe that you are primed and ready to live into your MIP. It's the sign that you are ready to join the club of maximum impact creators.

So how do you begin moving the kind of money that can actually create your Maximum Impact Potential?

You start by *owning your value.*

3 | TAKE YOUR SEAT AT THE TABLE

DURING MY TWENTIES, before my mom passed away, I taught fourth grade at the Allen Stevenson School in New York's Upper East Side. This was the kind of place where household names sent their children, and where it wasn't uncommon for the kids to be picked up from school in shiny black SUVs by private drivers. When I was hired, I felt like I'd hit the jackpot.

One year, the (very-well-connected) PTA brought in a

speaker to talk to the kids about overcoming obstacles. That speaker was none other than Emmanuel Ofosu Yeboah. At the time, he was in the middle of filming *Emmanuel's Gift*, a documentary about his life, with filmmakers Lisa Lax and Nancy Stern. The movie was narrated by Oprah Winfrey.

Emmanuel was born with a severely deformed right leg. In Ghana, where he grew up, I was told, any infant born with a disability was likely to be poisoned or left in the wilderness to die. Those who did survive were condemned to spend their lives locked away or begging on the streets. But Emmanuel's mother decided to go against that tradition.

I will never forget how he described, from the stage, having to hop from village to village on one leg. He learned to play soccer on one leg. He never gave up, no matter how many times others knocked him down.

One day, someone introduced him to the internet for the first time, and his life changed forever. They showed him how to search for answers to any question he had. And so, he made a decision to do what no one had ever done before: bike across his country one-legged! Rather than believe it was impossible, he made a powerful decision to do what it took to achieve his goal. He applied to an American sports foundation to send him a bike. That request was granted, and he set out to bike across Ghana to demonstrate that physical differences don't mean a damn thing when it comes to being a valuable member of society.

It worked. He got a boatload of media attention. He was the first disabled person to be invited to the Presidential Palace; previous to his work, people with disabilities were perceived as "cursed" and weren't allowed to enter. He rallied enough people to his cause that he was able to launch Ghana's first Paralympic team.

It's never easy to hold the attention of a group of elementary school kids, but Emmanuel had us riveted. At one point, he took off his prosthetic leg and passed it around the auditorium. Most of these kids had never seen one in real life.

One of the kids raised his hand and asked, "How old are you, anyway?"

"I am twenty-seven," Emmanuel replied.

I felt like I'd just had the wind knocked out of me. I was twenty-seven, too. And while I was sitting here in my preppy suit and tie, teaching math and reading to the sons and daughters of the elite, this man was literally changing a nation. If I was a ripple, he was a tsunami.

This, I realized, was a man who knew what he was worth in the world. He *owned his value*—not in a way that implied arrogance or conceit, but as a pure, simple fact of his existence. He knew that his life was just as important, just as meaningful, as that of anyone else on this planet—and he refused to accept any judgment, narrative, or cultural norm that tried to strip that from him.

"What's my excuse?" I wondered. "Why the hell am I not doing more to change the world? If he can do all that, coming from almost nothing and against those odds ..."

Now, I want to clarify that I hold the teaching profession in extremely high regard. Both my parents, my Aunt Linda, my Grandma Hilda, and my cousin, Megan, were educators, and I was proud to have followed in their footsteps. In fact, teaching was the first space where I really felt like I was making an impact—the first space I felt drawn to after my conversation with my eighty-year-old self yanked my feet off the banking path.

But I knew, as I witnessed Emmanuel captivate adults and kids alike with his courage and conviction, that teaching in a school wasn't where I was meant to make my biggest difference. The things I wanted to teach and learn weren't part of any curriculum—and by putting them aside, or trying to sneak my ideas in the back door during history lessons, I wasn't fully valuing myself and the contribution I was meant to make in the world.

If I stayed where I was, I wouldn't be owning my value. In fact, I'd be breaking the promise I'd made to my future self.

WHAT IT MEANS TO OWN YOUR VALUE

To me, the concept of "owning your value" is perfectly embodied by my late Aunt Linda.

Linda, like Emmanuel Ofosu Yeboah, was born with a severe leg deformation. She also had cerebral palsy. She walked with crutches for many years; eventually, her condition progressed to the point where she needed a wheelchair. By the end of her life, she was a quadriplegic, barely able to turn her head. She lived with her parents (my grandparents) for much of her adult life.

But here's the thing about Aunt Linda: her challenges never defined her.

She went to college. She traveled. She learned to drive. And she spent over three decades teaching kindergarten and first grade in public schools in Sodus, New York. She wanted to lift other people up—and for her, teaching was the best way to do that.

I can't even begin to number the challenges she faced every day. Once she was wheelchair bound, even using the bathroom became an obstacle. The wing of the school where her classroom was located didn't have a wheelchair-accessible bathroom, so she either had to make the trek across campus (not fun in the midst of a New York winter) or literally lever herself out of her wheelchair like Spiderman by bracing her arms against the sides of the stall. Her arms were like steel. One day, her arms gave out and she fell; this resulted in a frozen shoulder and caused her to "lose a wheel"—meaning, she could no longer push her own wheelchair. But even that couldn't stop her from teaching.

The school administration didn't want her to succeed. They micromanaged her. They treated her as "less than" the other, able-bodied teachers, even though her track record was stellar. Every summer, my cousins and I would help her decorate her classroom for the coming year with posters and supplies that she bought out of her own meager salary.

Aunt Linda was always given the hardest kids in the system. One was an African American kid named Brian who had been relegated by the system to the "dumb" track in kindergarten. She fought for him and believed in his capabilities. She saw his intelligence. By the end of the year, he was outperforming all the other kids in his class.

That kid, years later, started dating my cousin, Monica. They later married and had four beautiful, thoughtful children together. And when my grandparents died, Brian and Monica made the enormous commitment to do what no one else in the family could: they moved their family in with Aunt Linda so they could care for her.

I will never forget Brian's words to me: "Alok, Aunt Linda is never going to a nursing home as long as I live. She fought for me back then, and I will never abandon her." To her dying day, he stood by that promise.

Aunt Linda passed away in 2019. Everyone told her she wouldn't survive past the age of forty—but she outlived her parents, two of her siblings, and many of her peers. She had to give up so many dignities just to stay alive, but she knew her value in the world. She knew that she was changing lives as a teacher, an aunt, and a friend. She was a force for change even without legs that functioned.

Owning your value is about acknowledging that your very presence on this planet is a gift. You are here to make a difference, and you are just as worthy as the next person to make that difference.

When you can truly see this, feel it, and believe it, you become willing to take radical responsibility for your life. Like Aunt Linda, you become willing to see beyond all the evidence your circumstances are providing as "proof" of your non-validity, and instead position yourself to make the greatest possible impact with your unique gifts and talents.

Owning your value isn't the result of success, or connections, or brilliance. It's a powerful decision that only you can make. It's also a direct reflection of your worldview. You are either a victim, or you are a powerful creator. You can let circumstances, history, and other people dictate your value, or you can claim it for yourself. But you can't have it both ways.

In his book, *The Science of Being Great*, Wallace D. Wattles writes, "We must remember that this is not a bad world, but a good world in the process of becoming."

When you believe that the world is inherently a bad, scary, or broken place, you also make the decision to see yourself as inherently broken, because you are part of this world. Or, you might try to remove yourself from this world altogether, via a spiritual path that holds Heaven or enlightenment as the reward for suffering in this lifetime.

While it might *feel* true that our planet and society are broken, that way of thinking is a prison. It locks us into constantly working "against" what we perceive as wrong, rather than working "for" something that is better and right.

The alternative, of course, is to accept that our world is an inherently good place in the process of becoming better. When it comes to owning our value, this viewpoint is absolutely more aligned, because if the world is already beautiful and heading toward perfection, you can be a whole, beautiful part of it who is heading toward perfection, too.

Owning our value doesn't mean acting as though we are perfect. It doesn't mean becoming a delusional egomaniac who never admits to making mistakes. It doesn't mean making anyone else less than so we can be great. It's simply a movement from resistance to flow—from denying our inherent value, purpose, and gifts, to embracing and actually *using* them.

If you are reading this, you are capable of creating whatever change you want to see in the world.

If you are alive, if you are breathing, you are capable.

And if you're dead, you're still capable, because the ripple effect of you owning your value and living into your MIP will continue to spread even after you're gone.

Rest well, Aunt Linda. I don't know if you can see me now—but if you can, know that you were seen, and loved, and that your brilliance lives on in every child whose world you illuminated. Including mine.

RAISE YOUR DAMN HAND

Since you've read this far, I'm going to assume two things.

First, that you're at least marginally on board with the idea that true impact consciousness requires a monumental shift in your thinking. (If you weren't, you would have put down this book after Chapter 2.) And second, that you're willing to learn and do what it takes to realize your Maximum Impact Potential, even if it takes you to some uncomfortable places.

We're about to visit one of those places right now.

Owning your value means looking at the story you've internalized about who you are in the world. You know, the one that tells you what you can—and cannot—do, have, and be because of who you are and where you come from.

Yes, we're going there.

Every culture has its narratives. No matter where you go in the world (and I've spent time in over thirty countries on five continents), you'll come across tales of haves and have-nots, privilege and persecution. Every society has its own ideas about who is "worthy" of money, recognition, and respect. In America we have the "hard worker" narrative. In England it's how "old" your money is, and the particulars of your bloody accent. In India, it's the caste system, and the damaging narratives about karma and the privilege or punishment of your birth. For women in many cultures, it's an unattainable standard of beauty and giving to the point of servitude. For men in many cultures, it's about living up to a toxic and damaging standard of "manliness."

And yet, in every part of the world, in every time throughout history, there have been people who have radically contradicted these narratives. They are our heroes—the underdogs who succeed against all odds. Emmanuel Ofosu Yeboah is one. Oprah is another. (Come on. Do you really think those fat-cat television execs made it *easy* for a Black woman to build a talk show empire in the 80s? Not a chance.) Lisa Nichols went from welfare mom begging for diaper money to one of the most celebrated inspirational speakers on the planet. Ellen DeGeneres nearly lost it all when she came out as gay—but rather than give up, she changed the face of network TV. There was even that story about how Sly Stallone was so broke after he wrote *Rocky* that he had to sell his dog (turns out that wasn't true, but people ate it up anyway.)

Simply log into Netflix and you'll see how much we, as humans, love the narrative of success against incredible odds. So, doesn't it seem crazy that we worship the underdogs while at the same time telling ourselves (and other people) that we "can't" create the impact, income, and legacy we desire because we don't fit the acceptable tropes?

It makes no sense. And yet, we do this all the time.

We're too smart, but not genius enough. We're talented, but not talented enough. We're too "street," or not street enough. We're connected, but not connected enough. We're educated, but not educated enough. Even when we recognize our strengths, we immediately follow them with an excuse as to why they aren't enough to power us through adversity and into impact.

All of these excuses boil down to one simple but pervasive belief: that *we* aren't "enough."

This pattern is a more subtle version of the "DNA advantage" narrative I explored in Chapter 2, and it's just as patently false. After coaching hundreds of people from all kinds of backgrounds, I can say with certainty that nothing—and I mean *nothing*—can stand in your way when you truly commit to living your MIP.

You can either flush this down the toilet as a cliché platitude or accept it as a universal truth. Your choice.

I'm not denying that systemic racism exists. It does. I'm not denying that biases and stereotypes rear their ugly heads all the friggin' time, especially for people of color and LGBTQIA people. They do. I'm not denying that oppression and cultural silencing happen. They absolutely do.

What I *am* saying is that those things aren't actually what keep impact-makers like you from realizing their Maximum Impact Potential. No, in the end, the only thing that can put the brakes on your MIP is your belief that these systems, biases, and obstacles *are more powerful than you are.*

All of our beloved underdogs found ways to outcreate the systems and people who oppressed them. There's no reason we can't do the same. In fact, we *must*, because we will never change "the way things are" until we do what it takes to prove—to ourselves, and to the masses—that we can exist outside of that way of being. Accepting the status quo as inevitable only empowers the very systems, beliefs, and people that aim to oppress us.

I met Linda Hayles at a big coaching event in San Diego a few years ago. I don't recall how we started chatting, but I remember our conversation perfectly.

"Why are there not more people of color here?" she asked. "Why aren't there more people who look like us? Are we not the target market?"

"Of course we are," I replied. "You and I are here, aren't we?"

Linda understood immediately. We were there because we had *chosen* to be there. We had chosen to raise our hands and claim our seat at the table. We didn't make excuses or tell ourselves that we were unwelcome as people of color. We just showed up. The fact that there were only a few other brown-skinned people in the room was not a reflection on us.

Out of all the people I've ever worked with, Linda understands "just showing up" better than anyone. By owning her value and refusing to accept the narrative about what women like her can and cannot do, she's created a wildly successful coaching business focused on empowering ambitious entrepreneurs of all backgrounds to master high-ticket sales.

Linda was raised in a traditional, middle-class Puerto Rican household. Her parents were entrepreneurs and preachers—but even though Linda's mother ran her own business, the conversation in their home always revolved around a woman's place as a wife.

"It was always, 'Clean your room. No man wants a wife who's dirty. Don't sleep in. No man wants a lazy woman,'" Linda told me. "Everything in my narrative growing up was pointed toward me becoming a wife. So that's what I did."

Linda did become a wife and mother in her early twenties, but her marriage wasn't destined to be blissful. At the same time she was becoming a near-overnight success and top earner in her networking marketing company, she was dealing with intense physical, emotional, and financial abuse at home.

She said, "I had that awful moment where I realized, 'I have to own this.' I didn't deserve anything that happened to me. I didn't ask for it. But I kept *allowing* it because I was too scared to leave—and that didn't need to continue."

Radical personal responsibility has been a huge part of Linda's success. "I didn't have anyone in my family who was rich or successful. I didn't have any friends who were doing what I wanted to do. I didn't have the 'circle of influence' that would get me to where I wanted to go. But for twenty dollars, I could go to the bookstore and buy a book that would teach me everything I needed to know. I could listen to podcasts and watch YouTube videos for free. I realized that I was sick of trying to learn from my own mistakes. I wanted to start learning from other people's. That was how my self-definition began to change."

Today, Linda has turned her gift for sales and take-no-prisoners mindset into a multi-six-figure (and growing) business. She has redefined her relationship to money, success, and impact in ways she never could have imagined as a young woman, and she refuses to accept labels—of any kind—for herself or her clients. "There are perceived obstacles for everyone, but there are also very real ones that have to do with repetitive patterns. The things we hear over and over, the things we believe, the excuses we make, these are all part of a compound effect. We don't notice them right away, but they accumulate over time. That's what we're up against."

But, as Linda explains, we always have a choice. "We

don't have to shape ourselves around the labels. Black, Hispanic, Latina, victim, survivor ... They don't define us. But we have to heal. We can't speak from a wounded place. We need to do the work and then speak from our scars, so we can detach from the label and share the wisdom instead."

So, if you're waiting to claim your seat at the table, or take up the mantle of a torchbearer, remember ...

You are capable because you are human.

You are ready because you are here.

You are poised for impact because impact is what you are choosing *now*.

THE DOMINO EFFECT

Did you know that a single domino, when set in motion, generates enough force to knock over a domino 1.5 times its own size?

If you start with a domino the size of a Tic Tac, and keep increasing the domino size by 50 percent with each domino added, you will eventually generate enough force to knock over a domino the size of the Empire State Building.

When you choose to own your value and live into your Maximum Impact Potential, you are pushing over that first domino. Initially, the effects of what you're doing might feel small. Insignificant, even. But with every action you take, and every domino you topple, you are creating a ripple that will shake the world—as long as you are willing to keep that momentum going.

Imagine a world where everyone understands that *they* are the Tic Tac-sized domino, the initiator, the torchbearer. The world would be forever changed! Generational patterns would be broken. Harmful, extractive ways of making money would become extinct. Hopelessness would disappear.

When you understand the immense scale of your capacity for impact, you will see why even your small decisions matter when it comes to creating your MIP.

Even if you don't carry around any of the cultural and societal stories we explored above, you may still feel like you need to attain "giant" status (à la your favorite tech billionaire or celebrity coach) before you can initiate meaningful change in the world. This is false. Of course the Tic Tac won't do much against the Empire State Building if you put them right next to each other—but that doesn't mean that the Tic Tac has no power. It just needs to be properly *positioned* for impact.

Let's find out how to do that.

4 | THE EGO/ ETHOS TRAP

IN 2012, I CO-FOUNDED Fed by Threads, a supply-chain-aware, organic clothing company that provided more than 100,000 emergency meals through clothing sales.

I've always been obsessed with feeding people. (Today, it's my goal to provide one billion meals in my lifetime—but more on that later.) I was thrilled to be stepping into a visionary leadership role and making a huge difference—both in the textiles industry and in the daily lives of the people we were helping with food donations.

The thing was, at that time, I had no idea what it would take to move money through a mission, or how to create real value in the minds of the end users—aka, the people buying our clothes. I was a CEO, but I was still making decisions like an entrepreneur. This led to certain product decisions which were ethos-driven but not financially sound. I was so attached to creating my vision for the company that I was willing to sacrifice our financial stability.

There's a lot more to the story; what's relevant here is that my choices put the company in a very difficult situation. I ended up taking on outside investors and partners—all of whom had different ideas about how to manage the venture.

By 2016, we were experiencing fracture within the company; before too long, I found myself out of a job. As someone in the organization bluntly put it, "Alok, you have no friggin' idea what you're doing."

At first, things didn't look so bad. I had some savings. I figured I'd be okay until I managed to build my next "thing," whatever that might be. I convinced myself that this wasn't as big a deal as it seemed.

Then, the shit really hit the fan.

My son's mother, Jade, and I had been the sole signers on the lease for Fed By Threads' downtown Tucson retail location. When the new management of the company decided to close the location and take the company in a different direction, we were stuck with much of the responsibility for the lease. Suddenly, there was no more cushion. One thing after another fell apart. There were lawyers involved, and scary letters, and more stress than I've ever experienced before or since. Within a matter of a few weeks, I found myself living in a one-room studio apartment (a nice studio, to be clear, but still a single room) with no car, no money, and every credit card maxed out. I was a half-time single dad, struggling to provide—and it took every penny I had, plus some generous support from my friends Manish and Sean, to buy our way out of that lease.

So much for my big vision.

I felt like such a failure. I spent hours dissecting the events of the past few years, desperately trying to figure out where the heck I went wrong. Depression and anxiety gripped me. Some days, I could barely summon the energy to get out of bed, let alone contemplate my next visionary project.

And so, I started looking for jobs.

At first, my ego was a serious obstacle. I was still thinking of myself in the "visionary leader" stratosphere, when the reality was I was broke, broken, and mere weeks away from being homeless. There were jobs out there that matched my skill set, but I was too proud to apply for them. What would people think if I went from being the CEO of an impact-driven company—with a growing public reputation, a TEDx talk, and videos all over the internet—to the director of the local YWCA? And, worse, what if the YWCA *wouldn't take me*?

It was paralyzing.

As the weeks wore on, I started getting desperate. I prayed every night for a way out of this mess. "God, I will do *anything at all* to rise up out of this pit. I swear with my whole soul that if you show me the way, I'll do whatever it takes, and I will never go back to those old ways of being that put me here." It was a point of total surrender.

Almost immediately, the Universe delivered—although not in the way I was imagining.

My friend, Kristen Watts, had caught wind that I was in a tough spot. She called me and said, "Come over, I have an opportunity for you."

And so, a few days later, I found myself sitting on Kristen's brown couch, feigning confidence and acting like I was "casually open" to hearing her offer. I knew she knew I was up shit's creek—but I couldn't quite let go of my pride enough to talk about it.

"I can get you an interview with my company," Kristen said as we settled onto her plush brown couch. "The job is way below your level, but I think you need to take it, because this company is actually built for you. You're their ideal customer—but since you don't have the money to hire them right now, this is the next best thing. As part of the offer, I can get you full access to all the video trainings we give our customers. At night, you can study and train and retool yourself."

Sensing my hesitation, she continued, "You can work from home. No one will have to know. But I promise, this company is totally aligned with who you are and what you value."

The company? Lucrative Luminary, founded by Callan Rush and Justin Livingston.

The position? Front line customer service.

The pay? Twenty bucks an hour.

My ego, of course, rebelled. How could I go from running a whole company to answering phones and doing data entry? I started seesawing between wanting that paycheck and believing I could just go launch my next mission-driven company (with no money and a battered belief in myself). Clearly I hadn't gotten punched in the face enough yet.

When I told my son's mom that I was thinking about declining the opportunity, she looked me square in the eye, and said, "Enough already. It's time to get over yourself and get a fucking job."

Sometimes the hardest things to hear are the things we need to hear the most. I will always be grateful to Jade for taking a stand for me in that moment. The truth was, my decisions no longer just affected my life: they impacted her and my son, too.

I had promised God I would do whatever it took. And

so, I swallowed my pride and asked Kristen to get me an interview.

It was like pulling a release valve on the tension in my soul. It would be nice, I thought as I walked back to my lonely studio, to have a paycheck. To be able to buy groceries without stress. To have time to get back on my feet and find my next big idea.

Then came the interview.

My prospective employers started with a DISC assessment. The response? "We can't hire you for this position. You have the same profile as our CEO."

In response, I did something I'd never done before in my life: I begged.

I *begged* for that twenty-dollar-an-hour job. I begged to be a part of their company. I said, "I just want you to give me finite tasks, and let me do them really, really well. Please, give me a chance."

Finally, Kristen stepped in on my behalf, and assured my interviewer, "I know him. He means what he says. And if he doesn't," she added with a smirk, "you can fire him."

Before I took that position, I didn't know the coaching industry even existed. I mean, I'd heard of Tony Robbins, but that was about it. I had no clue what I was stepping into. But Kristen had seen something for me, and I was willing to trust the direction in which she—and God—were clearly pointing me.

And so, I worked the phones all day from the corner desk in my studio. I became a rock star customer service agent. And, the crazy thing was, I actually enjoyed the work.

After putting my son to sleep at night, I studied. I learned about mindset, and how our thoughts create our reality. I learned about marketing, and how to create aligned and powerful messages. I learned about coaching relationships, and why asking for help is the bravest thing we can ever do as visionary leaders. In short, I learned all the stuff I wished I had known when I was running Fed by Threads—and began to get a sense of where I'd gone wrong in that role.

Within a couple of months, I was invited to attend one of the company's live events. It was basically unpaid; they would cover my room and meals, but I wouldn't get an hourly rate. I was like, "I'll be there!" I was over the moon to get to witness from the inside how to run a three-day, 300-person event. I didn't care what I had to do. "I'll run that friggin' mic around the room if that's what you need," I told my supervisor.

At that event, I witnessed a million dollars in sales transactions unfold in a matter of a few hours. Twenty people signed up for the company's $50,000 offer.

I thought, "I want to do that. I *can* do that."

Eventually, I transitioned from customer service to the sales team. I closed about $250,000 in deals within a couple of weeks. I was on fire.

But then, the company folded.

They let 75 percent of their employees go in one day. I got an additional six weeks. They did everything with real grace and clarity. They tried to find new positions for all of us—and because I'd demonstrated that I was great at sales, they gave me a referral to a woman named Suzanne Evans, who took me on as a hired gun on her sales team. I will forever be grateful to her for giving me a chance.

Within a couple weeks, they threw me in the fire at a 500-person live event. Without really knowing all that much about the client's business or programs, I closed about $175,000 of business.

The fact that I was good at this "sales stuff" kind of blew my mind. After all, I'd had such a challenging experience selling my mission and vision as a CEO. What was different now?

What came through was a lesson that rocked my world.

SOLVE THE PROBLEMS PEOPLE ACTUALLY HAVE

In Fed by Threads, I was focused on solving issues I was passionate about. I was committed to creating sustainable clothing with minimal environmental impact, and to ending hunger. The fact that I could do these things while also producing a cool, functional product was a bonus.

The thing was, my philanthropic goals weren't "problems" for my customers.

Sure, they cared about the environment and other humans ... in a theoretical sort of way. But because I wasn't customer-focused in my marketing and business strategy, buying my clothes didn't give people the satisfaction of having solved a problem for *themselves*.

Whenever I asked customers for feedback on our clothes, the first thing they said was, "I love how soft they are!" (That's the beauty of bamboo and organic cotton, by the way.) They didn't talk about how many gallons of water were saved in the production of their new tee shirt. They didn't talk about "made in America" or "sweatshop free." They weren't gushing to their friends about my lofty mission. They talked about the way the clothes felt on their skin.

If only I had focused on selling The Softest Clothes on the Planet, I'd probably still be running that company to this day. Why? Because "softness" and "comfort" were real problems I could solve for my buyers. The ethos—the "impact" part that mattered to me—was just the cherry on top.

Far too many visionaries fall into the trap of trying to sell what matters to *them*, instead of what matters to the people who are buying from them. This is true in every industry, from product development to coaching and professional services. They think that because something feels profound in their world, it should feel that way to their customers, too. The result is that their messaging doesn't land. By being too attached to their ideas about what other people should know or be doing, they actually alienate the very people they're trying to serve. This creates a bottleneck in the money moving through their missions and cripples their ability to create the impact they desire.

I've seen coaches do this by trying to sell transformation according to their own breakthroughs rather than those their clients need. I've seen thought leaders do this by treating their ethos, rather than their outcome, as the core selling point of their product. I've seen nonprofits do this by refusing to craft their messaging to solve a "problem" for their donors.

Newsflash: "I think this matters, so you should too" isn't good enough to get people to open their wallets. And, as we've discovered ... no money, no mission.

All of those social impact superheroes we talked about in Chapter 2 knew this secret, too. Mother Teresa was said to laugh in the faces of billionaires who didn't give enough to her cause. By reminding them of how their peers would perceive these paltry gifts, she convinced them to write checks ten times the size they had intended ... and feel great about doing it. She gave them what they wanted, which was status. Martin Luther King, Jr. convinced his donors of the value of being on the right side of history. If he had come from the perspective of "everyone should see how important this is," they would never have been able to fund their movements. In essence, they had to learn to sell the *feeling their funders wanted to experience* in order to finance the change they wanted to see in the world.

When I started mainlining training modules at night after working the full day shift, this truth started to unfold for me. People won't pay you for your idealism. But they *will* pay you to solve their most pressing problems.

I saw this even more clearly while working with Suzanne Evans and other big names in the transformation industry. They are masters at illuminating the "gap"—the space between where someone is and where they want to be. They position their products as bridges to get people across that divide.

In 2018, the truth became clear at last. The path to creating my Maximum Impact Potential was to teach *this*.

The minute this knowledge landed, I had a full-on tantrum. "Are you kidding me, God?" I raged. "You showed me the way out of all of this, just so I could be a *sales coach*? How can I have any pride? Look at everything I've done! This isn't visionary leadership!"

In truth, the thought of calling myself a "sales coach" made me feel embarrassed and ashamed. What would people say? Would they judge me for my fall from grace? What would my intellectual father think of me?

And then a mentor asked me one powerful question:

"Alok, how many people do you know who want to make a positive impact in the world but struggle to position, sell, and close potential deals, and eventually burn out and quit?"

I instantly pictured many such people in my mind, and knew the answer: "Almost all of them."

Suddenly, it was clear. The very skill I had honed for years—ever since those days hitting the pavement with Uncle Jim—but was ashamed to possess ... this was exactly the skill too many impact-driven leaders lacked.

In my soul, I knew sales was *rocket fuel* for every great idea to uplift humanity. It was the missing piece that was keeping visionary leaders from succeeding in their efforts to change the world. If you can't sell, you can't serve.

A coach named Cole Gordon passed along this simple idea to me: "Business is the act of solving somebody else's problem. Money follows value, so sales is simply the ability to communicate the fact that you solve a problem."

When the problem you solve matters to the people who need it solved, they will pay you. And when people pay you, money moves through you—through your ideals, your mission, and your vision for yourself and the world.

My ego, plus my unwillingness to position my products according to what people valued (instead of what *I* had decided they should value) had cost me everything. It was a brutal learning experience. But now, I had a way to leverage that learning to create value for others.

The more value you create for other people, the more you increase your Maximum Impact Potential. You tap into the unending supply available to all of us—and you can use that supply to power the change you want to create. (Whatever your opinion of Bill Gates, Jeff Bezos, or other billionaire founders, you have to acknowledge that there's a hell of a lot of money moving through the missions they've chosen!)

Conversely, when you try to force the market to see through your lens of value, you stagnate your Maximum Impact Potential, because only a few die-hards who think the same way you do will value your work enough to pay for it.

If you're committed to reaching your Maximum Impact Potential in your lifetime, let go of your attachment to *your* ideas about what matters, and find a way to serve the people you want to serve *in a way that matters to them.*

Be aware that, if you're anything like me, your sweet spot for "problem solving" and money flow might not be exactly where you think it is. We'll talk more about this in upcoming chapters—but for now, just drop your attachments for a few hours or days. Stop asking "What do I want," and start asking, "What problems do my clients (or potential clients) need solved?" Soon, you'll start to see how you can actually start to move money through your mission.

Today, I'm having a bigger impact in the spaces that matter to me than ever before. Not as the visionary CEO of an environmentally-conscious company, but as a *sales coach*. How? Because there's money flowing through my mission now. My ethos attracts my ideal clients—but I'm no longer trying to sell them on *my* MIP. Instead, I'm creating real impact by helping them find theirs.

The best part of this story, though, is that my company, Uplift Millions, has now redirected cash flow from the coaching business to launch a sustainable clothing company that empowers women. We are also moving into regenerative farming to fight climate change, and are prepping to enter other industries. In short, becoming a "sales coach" has birthed the Impact Empire I always dreamed of.

AN EPIDEMIC OF HUMBLENESS AND A PLAGUE OF EGO

There are two common traits in visionary leaders that sabotage their ability to create impact over and over again: *false humbleness* and *unchecked ego*. Believe it or not, these two things can and do exist in the same space at the same time.

When I was growing up, I could never take a compliment. I had a lot going for me. I was smart and good-looking. I was musically gifted. I could sing. I was a good soccer player. And I cringed every time someone recognized me for any of these things.

It wasn't that I didn't know I was good at stuff. It was that, when people acknowledged my talents, it put me in a spotlight I hadn't asked for. And no matter what I said in response, it always felt like the wrong decision.

Having grown up in an extended family that was half Brahman and half Christian, I had a lot of screwed up ideas about pride and self-worth. On the one hand, there was the Indian side of me, where caste and birth were treated as a reward or punishment from the gods. On the other hand, my Christian relatives talked about "humbleness," and referred to pride as a deadly sin—right up there with murder, theft, and adultery.

Then, of course, there was my ego—the part of me that wanted to be seen as good, kind, and worthy in others' eyes. In my world, at that time, that meant being humble, and not getting too big for my britches.

Honestly, I'm not surprised that compliments made me want to run for my life.

So, I deflected. I credited the team for the win, even though I was the captain and had created the field strategy. I credited the chorus when I was the soloist. I shrugged off my good grades, saying that the course was easy.

Finally, my mother sat me down for a chat. "Alok, how do you feel when you give someone a present?"

"Um, good?"

"Now, what if you gave someone a gift that you had chosen just for them, but the minute you handed them the box, they set it aside and said, 'I don't deserve this. I'm going to give it to my friend instead'?"

I wasn't sure where this was going, so I said nothing.

My mother sighed. "When you deflect a compliment, you're doing the same thing. You're taking someone's gift and giving it away. You're robbing them of the joy of giving their praise. So, from now on, whenever someone says something kind, you are only going to say two words. 'Thank you.'"

When we deflect praise or refuse to acknowledge what we have accomplished, we aren't doing the world, or our Maximum Impact Potential, any favors. Why? Because we are backpedaling out of the energetic flow the Universe/ God is trying to create to align with and support our vision. Essentially, we're saying, "I don't want to own my value, or the value of what I've created in the world."

Martyrdom is a huge badge of honor in the impact community, but it's killing your MIP. Stop thinking of yourself as a "servant" to the cause. You're not a servant. You're a powerful creator. Service and servitude are *not* the same thing.

This internal shift also influences how we perceive and digest failure. When we are powerful creators, we can move from a language of "failure" as an ending to failure as a learning opportunity. Not everything works. Not everything that works, works the first time. If you make failure final, and never move on to that second round (or third, or fourth), you will never see the opportunities for growth that failure presented. If I had been just a little bit more trapped in my ego in 2016, I could have ended up in a very different place.

Owning your failures is part of owning your value. When you allow the bumps, splats, and full-out face-plants to become part of the journey, instead of obstacles to it, you will learn faster, recover faster, and increase your MIP.

If you don't own your value, you will never receive in full proportion to the value you provide. And when you can't receive in proportion, money won't flow through your mission, and you will always struggle to create the impact you envision. No matter how many Tic Tac-sized dominoes you have, if that's *all* you have, you will never knock over the Empire State Building. You have to be willing to expand, and own that expansion every step of the way.

I've had many conversations with highly spiritual people who talk about the smallness of humanity—the fact that we are mere specks of dust in the immensity of the Universe, and that, ultimately, we only think we matter because our ego needs to believe in our "mattering" to preserve itself.

I disagree. If we are specks, we are specks of awesome-ness—of dynamite. We have the gift of consciousness. We can *move matter* with our thoughts, our commitments, and our aligned actions. We can be the domino that sets a million other dominoes in motion. Every one of us has that poten-tial, if only we are willing to position ourselves properly for impact. Therefore, I believe it's a disservice to the omnipres-ent force of God/Universe to say, "I don't matter because

I'm just a little speck of nothingness." In fact, when you do that, you're deflecting the biggest compliment you will every receive—the compliment, and the gift, of your *existence*.

So, my friend, just stop it with the false humility. You know you're great at what you do. You know the value you want to bring forward in the world. Stop deflecting, minimizing, and undercutting your work and your impact. When someone gushes over how you've changed their life, just say two words:

"Thank you."

POSITIONING FOR IMPACT

Having read what I've shared so far, you may be starting to re-imagine the path you've chosen for creating impact in the world.

(This is good. It's important to "fact-check" ourselves every once in a while to make sure we are still operating in alignment with our Maximum Impact Potential.)

Positioning for impact requires you to do three things.

1. Own your value
2. Decide which problems you will solve for people
3. Decide how you will get paid to solve those problems

As my story illustrates, we get into trouble when our ego gets too attached to what we think our path to impact *should* be. Our hearts are in the right place, and that's awesome. But our ideas about what *we* want are actually irrelevant. What matters is what people need from you.

I've seen so many visionaries make this mistake. They believe their product or service will change lives, so instead of testing the market, they pour their heart and soul into it, design the heck out of it, bring it to market, and then—

Crickets.

Sooner or later, they figure out that either they've missed the mark completely, or the market simply wasn't ready for what they were creating. This is devastating. How much time, money, and energy could have been saved if they had stopped asking, "How do *I* want to make an impact?" and instead asked, "What do people *need* from me right now?"

This is the shift in thinking that will take you out of your ego and onto what Keith J. Cunningham calls, "The road less stupid"—and what I call the road to maximum impact.

Owning your value doesn't mean that you continue to push your own agenda despite the resistance (crickets). It means that you fully believe in the value of who you are as a human—a cosmic speck of awesomeness—and that you commit to bringing the full force of your gifts, talents, skills, and knowledge to bear *no matter what problem you are currently getting paid to solve.* Your value will follow you no matter where you go, because it was never separate from you in the first place.

I'm not saying you should compromise your integrity to make money. I'm saying that finding a problem you can solve for others to help them improve their lives (and the planet) is the best way to get money moving through your mission.

When you restructure your thinking in this way, you may find that solving an urgent problem for others allows you to create *more* positive impact than the thing you were previously attached to. When that happens, you'll be amazed that you didn't see it before.

Finding the problem you want to solve may also inspire another question: "Do I desire to make my biggest impact through the existing infrastructure in my life, or do I need to create a new one?" (By "infrastructure," I mean your current company, job, or professional role.)

In order to own your value and solve others' problems in a way that will align with your MIP, do you stay where you are? Do you step into a new level or type of leadership within your company or organization? Do you have the power to steer your current ship in a new direction?

If, like most of my clients, you're an entrepreneur, the answer to this will usually be, "Hell, yes!" You may need to realign your offers and start thinking of yourself as a CEO rather than a solo operator—but the choice is in your hands. You're free to run with whatever you uncover as you own your value and align your service with the needs of the market.

If you're currently operating as an intrapreneur (a professional inside someone else's company), however, this question may be more complicated. Do you need to climb the ladder into the C-suite? Do you need to make a lateral move to a more aligned organization? Do you need to jump ship and start your own company?

No answer is right or wrong, but you need to be willing to ask powerful questions like, "Can my existing infrastructure support and facilitate the fullest expression of my MIP?" If yes, it's time to get bold and courageous, and start leading in a new direction. If not, you'll need to make a plan to transition out of where you are and start building something that is more aligned for you.

One of the best examples I've seen of this type of realignment came from Adam Goodman, the third-generation CEO of Goodman's Office Furniture. He was the keynote at the Social Entrepreneurship Summit in Phoenix, Arizona several years ago, at which I was a panelist. When he took the stage, I expected to be bored to tears—I mean, how could office furniture *not* be boring?—but when he started speaking, I was glued to the edge of my seat.

Goodman shared the story of why he decided to take the office furniture and supply company founded by his grandfather through the rigorous process of B-Corp certification.

He told us, "I knew if I didn't reposition our brand to be more sustainable and socially-focused, it wouldn't be a problem today. It wouldn't be a problem next year. But in twenty, or fifty, or a hundred years? We would no longer have a company."

Goodman realized that the fastest track to stay relevant to both his customers and his evolving work force was to change the infrastructure—in this case, the culture of his company—to attract quality workers and preserve natural resources. And so, he made a powerful decision to leverage his influence as CEO to make a sharp right turn, redesign his entire business for impact, and radically uplevel both his own MIP and those of all his future employees.

So, right now, ask yourself: "What changes, if any, are required so that my infrastructure can support my Maximum Impact Potential?"

WHAT'S BURIED WITHIN YOU?

Depending on where you are right now, you might be ready to take what I just shared and run with it. Or, you might need to pause and figure out how you can realign your products, offers, or audience to solve that urgent problem and start linking income to your impact. My advice is to take your time with this, and find the help and coaching you need to get clear before you take action.

Or, you might be realizing that your current industry isn't aligned with owning your value and creating your Maximum Impact Potential. Rather than pause and realign, you might be tempted to scrap everything and go looking for a new purpose.

Before you set off down that road, let me tell you about my first apartment, which I bought when I was twenty-three. It was on the sixth floor in a pre-war building across the street from the Brooklyn Museum of Art. It had only a half-kitchen, no view, and was only 500 square feet, but I sensed I had struck gold. I borrowed money from my parents for the down payment, and my teaching salary at the time was just enough to qualify for a mortgage.

One night after I had moved in, my mom stood by one of the closet door frames and asked, "Do you have a knife?"

Confused, I started digging in my piles of moving boxes, and finally came up with a steak knife. She snatched it out of my hand and started cutting into thick layers of paint on the doorway.

"What are you doing?" I asked frantically.

"Something tells me there's steel under there. Hand me a magnet." Sure enough the magnet clamped right on. She continued: "If you want to add a ton of value to this apartment, strip off all this old paint and reveal the steel." (Yes, certain gender norms were reversed in my family. My dad taught me everything I know about cooking, and my mom taught me about renovations and automobile maintenance.)

And so, I followed her advice. It took a wire brush, noxious chemicals, and weeks of elbow grease to get rid of an absurd number of layers of old Brooklyn paint, but Mom was right; the steel frames were gorgeous.

Eventually I started working on the bedroom door and came across an odd two-inch bubble in the paint. As I sanded the paint off, I discovered a small *mezuzah*, a Jewish prayer scroll that some set of former residents had hung there. It's meant to be touched to invoke a blessing as people walk in the door.

How amazing, I marveled. *After all these decades, there was this hidden blessing buried here, just waiting for me to uncover it.*

Your purpose, your reason for being on this planet, is like that *mezuzah*. It's been encoded into you. It's always been there, even if it's been buried under layers of paint and experience. You might not be able to see and remember it—yet—but you will.

As you consider how to position yourself for impact and get money flowing through your mission, remember that your purpose and impact potential are never external. You don't need to find them; they're already there. Instead, ask "What beliefs do I need to remove in order to uncover my Soul Mission?"

And then, get ready for what I like to call the "shit pile

removal expedition."

Most of us, at some point, will realize that we have been living someone else's dream or expectation, rather than our own—that we've been living under layers of paint that someone else put there. For me, this happened when I realized that teaching elementary school wasn't the highest and best path for me. It happened again when I had to adapt my definition of "visionary leader" to include sales coaching and the monumental impact I could have in that space.

You have a totally unique skill set. Some of that is your natural gifts and talents—the way you're designed as a speck of awesomeness. Some you've acquired through the various jobs, experiences, and relationships you've had throughout your life. But your purpose doesn't depend on your toolkit. In fact, your toolkit may be part of the paint that's hiding your purpose from view.

Earlier in my life, I had a false belief that I could either use my toolkit to get rich at all costs or I could go into the social impact field (read, nonprofits) and earn squat. That was an old paradigm. Service and wealth are not diametrically opposed; in fact, as we've learned, they are inseparable. When I figured out how to use my skills to get rich in accordance with my values of integrity, service, and equity while solving a problem for people whose work I believed in, everything aligned and expanded. Those dominoes started scaling in ways I'd never even known were possible.

Chances are, your purpose or Soul Mission—the one you've been searching everywhere for—lives at that intersection of your skills and values. You don't need to sacrifice your integrity to make money. You don't need to set aside impact to earn millions. In fact, you can't. And if that problem you want to solve requires skills that aren't in your toolkit yet? Just go learn them. Better yet, hire someone who knows them. Once you make the decision to operate as you were designed to do as a unique expression of God/ Universe, nothing is out of your reach—especially not the purpose for which you were designed.

Close your eyes and ask, "What is the big, juicy problem I came to Earth to solve (or at least reduce)? If there was no way I could fail, what solution would I want to contribute to?" This powerful question can be like a guiding star for you when you feel uncertain.

Imagine what it will feel like when you stand in *that* place—the place where all the parts of you meet in service to yourself, your family, your community, and the planet. The place where you will generate such power for change that your legacy will continue to move mountains long after you are dust. The place where you feel purposeful, powerful, and unstoppable. The place where your Maximum Impact Potential can multiply.

Let's go there.

PART II

BECOME
A WEALTH
CIRCULATOR

5 | CIRCLES OF CONTRIBUTION

WHEN I WAS A KID, my mom would often take a satchel full of oranges with her when we left our family's residence in India.

In Delhi, Bombay, and pretty much anywhere else we went, there were always kids coming up to us begging for help. If we were in the car, they would tap on the windows. If we were on the street, they would clutch at our pant legs.

It was devastating to witness. I can't even imagine how

devastating it must have been to live.

I wanted to give them rupees, because I figured money would help them get things they needed—like food. But soon I realized that, even if I brought every rupee from my allowance, plus what I could beg off my relatives, I wouldn't have enough to help them all.

My mother hit on the idea of oranges because they were easy to buy in bulk and provided immediate food for those hungry kids. And so, we would set out together on whatever errand was necessary that day: her lugging the satchel, me passing out the fruit.

No matter how many oranges we packed, we never had enough.

I started to wonder, "How can I give more? How can I find more oranges? How can I earn more rupees?" I lay in bed thinking about the awful poverty I'd witnessed that day, and the day before, and the day before that. Suddenly, I had the heartbreaking realization that I could give away everything I had, everything my family had, everything our friends had ... and there would still not be enough oranges.

And then, after all that we had was gone, my family would be homeless and begging for oranges, too.

Those early experiences were the origin of my desire to feed people as a part of my impact strategy. I also think they're part of why I was drawn to the banking world as a teenager. After all, with more money, we can solve more problems, right?

Well, yes ... and no.

When we discover the space where we are aligned to make an impact, our instinct is often to give it all away, all at once. I once had a client tell me, "I want to give away 50 percent of what I earn to help struggling women."

"Are you opening a charity?" I asked her.

"No. I want to use 50 percent of my gross profits from coaching to help these women. I only need to make enough to cover my bills."

All I could do was shake my head.

"What? Do you think I'm not giving enough?" she asked.

"I think that's a recipe for disaster," I said. "You need to increase what you're currently bringing in by a factor of ten before you give away that kind of percentage."

You may be confused. Aren't we talking about Maximum Impact Potential here?

Yes, but hear me out.

In order to be a true impact-maker, you need to *take care of yourself first*—and I don't just mean in a "pay this month's bills" kind of way. You need to build reserves that you can then leverage for greater impact, and position yourself to give from a place of wholeness and stability.

You will *always* perceive that there is more you can do to uplift other people. Your passion and drive to rewrite the status quo is part of what will power your Maximum Impact Potential. But if you fall into the trap of feeding the hungry maw of human need with everything you have, from day one, you will *never* be able to scale your impact. You will start every day from ground zero. And before too long, you will go from giving oranges to begging for them.

THE FOUR CIRCLES OF CONTRIBUTION

What's the first thing you hear every time you get on an airplane? "In case of emergency, secure your own oxygen mask before helping others."

The same is true when it comes to money and impact.

Despite the urgency you may feel to make a difference *now*, it's vital to understand that impact is a long game. The longest game. A game that, if played well, will outlive you by decades or even centuries—but here and now, it requires you to put yourself first.

So please, before you drain your entire bank account to buy oranges, or give away 50 percent of your gross profit before you even take a salary (I'm still shaking my head at that one), take off the martyr goggles and have a good, hard look at where you're standing. If all you have right now are a few Tic Tac-sized dominoes, it will be a lot harder to knock down a wall.

Your impact is a ripple. It starts with *you impacting you*, and spreads from there to include your family, your community, and eventually the planet. Until you are taken care of—until you are *abundant*—your impact will never grow beyond where it is right now.

The Four Circles of Contribution

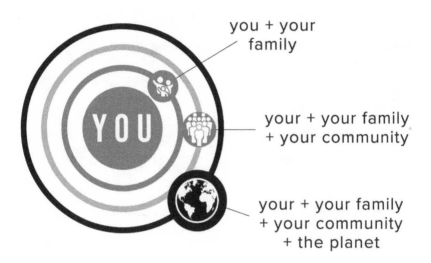

you + your family

your + your family + your community

your + your family + your community + the planet

The Four Circles of Contribution are based on how much money you currently have flowing through you in the present moment.

When you merge your transformational skill or product with the needs of the market, as we covered in Chapter 4, money will begin to flow to you. But it should only flow out *from* you in proportion to the Circle of Contribution you currently occupy. In essence, your Circle tells you how many oranges you can afford to give away while still increasing your impact trajectory.

Let's break down the Four Circles one by one.

CIRCLE 1: YOU

It's time to get real about your financial situation. Do you actually make enough to provide for your own needs?

Don't feed me that line about, "I just need enough to cover my bills." That's a joke. Most people I coach don't even know what their true cost of living is.

For example:

- Do you have a retirement plan that will replace your ideal income, or do you plan to work until you're ninety (and hope that Social Security still exists by then)?
- Do you have comprehensive health insurance? How about an HSA?
- Do you have outstanding loans and/or credit card debt?
- Can you afford a home that feels like a truly safe, creative, and abundant space?
- Are you still compromising your ideal standard of living (or, conversely, are you living beyond your means)?
- Can you do the things that nourish your mind, body, and spirit on a regular basis, or are they "treats" you give yourself when you have some extra cash?

- Do you feel fully supported in *all* aspects of life—or are you hanging on by a thread?

If you don't have an *actual* surplus from your business or salary each month, please don't try to put money toward global impact just yet. You'll end up on a hamster wheel of burnout in no time. Instead, focus on building your impact close to home. Create what *you* need so you can give from overflow down the road.

Some general guidelines: If you are making less than $5,000/month in your business, or if you earn a salary of less than $60,000, you are in Circle 1. If you're like more than 70 percent of American households, you are one bad accident, hospital stay, or business failure away from bankruptcy—and if that happens, how will you save the world? Your MIP depends on you being stable and supported.

I'm not saying you can't make an impact in Circle 1. My Aunt Linda never made it out of this financial Circle, and she changed hundreds of lives. However, when we're focused on MIP, a granular, one-person-at-a-time impact may not feel like enough. We want to do *big* things—and so we get ahead of ourselves when we don't yet have the financial flow to make those big things sustainable. If this is where you're at right now, don't give up. You *will* have an impact simply by doing what you do, and being who you are. Focus on owning your value, and give your time, energy, and attention rather than money right now.

CIRCLE 2: YOU + YOUR FAMILY

Once your needs are provided for, you can start looking at how you can contribute to your family. If you have a partner and/or kids, consider the following:

- Does your combined household income support your ideal lifestyle?
- Does every member of your household have adequate health, dental, mental, and physical support?
- Do you have college savings plans?
- Do you have an emergency fund and savings to fall back on if something goes awry?
- Does everyone in your family have the freedom and resources to freely pursue their passions and interests (sports, dance, art, music, travel, etc.)?
- Do you want to build a legacy or trust for your children, grandchildren, or other family members?

It's not selfish to take care of your family first. In fact, it's the *only* way you will be able to give sustainably beyond your household. I can't tell you how often I see people priding themselves on making a difference in the world when they can't even provide adequately for their own kids. They convince themselves that sacrificing their family's wellbeing is just collateral damage for "doing the good work." In other words, they're giving away all of their oranges. Not okay.

Financial stress creates generational patterns of scarcity, lack, and perceived powerlessness, and is a top killer of relationships. If you can rewrite those narratives within your own family, you have a chance to change hundreds of lives through many generations to come. So don't discount the impact of providing better security, opportunities, and money consciousness for your loved ones. As a provider, you are empowering their MIPs, too.

Also, as I mentioned in the section on Circle 1, you will absolutely have an impact every day through your work and relationships while you are moving through this Circle. It will simply happen more through your time, energy, and attention than through your money flow at this stage.

General guideline: If you are earning less than $10k/ month in your business or career, keep your attention close to home.

CIRCLE 3: YOU + YOUR FAMILY + YOUR COMMUNITY

Once you've created abundance for yourself and your family, it's time to spread it into the community.

You can do this through charitable giving, job creation in your impact-focused business, micro-lending and venture capital for local businesses, or any other close-to-home opportunities that you feel called to explore.

At this stage, your household income will be greater than $15,000 per month. Remember, this is about giving from overflow. Consider devoting a percentage of your earnings to your community and watch your impact catch fire!

CIRCLE 4: YOU + YOUR FAMILY + YOUR COMMUNITY + THE PLANET

Global impact takes cash flow. Once you've provided for your family and begun to create impact in your community, you can begin to consider global impact.

Some ways you can do this are:

- Give substantive monthly cash donations to organizations that matter to you. (At the time of this writing, I plant 10,000 trees a month, feed 10,000 meals a month, and end blindness for fifty people through cash contributions to organizations I believe in.)

- Establish your own charity and fund it with a percentage of profits from your business.

- Become your own "bank" through microlending to cottage businesses and startups around the world.

At this stage, your household income will be greater than $250,000 a year. Your investments into impact will continue to compound, and you will see your vision for global impact come to life. You will literally be building an Impact Empire (more on that later).

START IN THE CENTER

Too many impact-driven people are trying to do things in reverse order. They want to save the world—and then (maybe) claim some scraps for themselves. They're trying to play in Circle 4 when they haven't mastered Circle 1.

Reality check: your ambition to save the world doesn't mean shit if you can't take care of your own household. Sooner or later, you're going to run out of oranges—and it's you and your family, not the world at large, who will pay the price.

You have a choice. You can give everything away today, and essentially flatline your financial flow and MIP. Or, you can focus on your current circle of contribution and grow within it and beyond it, until you're ready to become a *wealth circulator*—a channel for money and impact that can scale exponentially with time, just like those perpetually-increasing dominoes.

Again, this doesn't mean that you can't have meaningful impact in every Circle, and at every stage of life, or that you will never realize your MIP if you don't get rich. You can still impact people every day, in amazing ways. But if you're actually out to change the world, scale your impact, and create a *movement*, you will see greater and more far-reaching results if you follow this model.

We'll talk more about the idea of wealth circulation in the next chapter—but for now, ask yourself, "What circle am I currently in—and what will it take for me to move outward from here?"

ADMIT IT, YOU LIKE MONEY

When you own your value and move into that sweet spot of monetizing your knowledge and solving problems in the marketplace, you *will* start to attract money. And, if you're anything like most impact-driven people I know, you may immediately feel ashamed about it.

Let's take the gloves off, my friend.

You like money. Admit it.

I like money, too. In fact, I *love* money. I love how flowing money through my Circles of Contribution makes me feel. I love using money to further the causes I feel passionate about. I love investing in other impact-driven businesses around the world. I love everything about money.

And yet, when I say, "I love money," people think I'm a greedy prick.

Money is the lifeblood of positive change. Everything you want to do is in some way dependent on your ability to move flows of money. More, as you've seen, your ability to flow money corresponds directly to your Maximum Impact Potential. You don't get to the outermost Circle of Contribution without learning how to play full-out in the financial realm.

I want you to understand that there is no shortage of money. Money is *energy*, and energy is omnipresent. It can be neither created nor destroyed, it can only flow and change state. If you decide it should flow toward and through you, it will. If you decide it should flow away from you, it will. But it will continue to flow regardless of how much you judge it.

I visualize this as a "money river." We can either be paddling upstream, against the current (i.e., trying to create impact while fighting with money flows), or we can let the river carry us toward bigger and better things. Either way, though, we need to get wet.

Our society has mastered the art of luring people to want more money but then shaming them for that very desire. It's like the collective is saying, "Come to the river—but shame on you if you actually take a dip!" Many of us who grew up in middle- or working-class families carry a fear that accumulating money will somehow taint us or cause us to become like *those people*. So, we flipflop between wanting to make more money and hating the idea of being rich. It's like turning a faucet on and off. Money—the water—doesn't care. It's still there in abundance whether the tap is on or off.

Money, in and of itself, has no power over human consciousness. It's not the root of all evil. It's not a savior. It's just energy. And when you add energy to anything—including a human being—that energy will illuminate and amplify what was already there.

If you are a good person who wants to create a positive impact in the world, money will amplify that desire and potential. You will be, and do, more good because you have more money.

If you are already an asshole, well ... money will definitely make you a bigger asshole—so maybe you'll want to work on that.

If you don't like the way that "rich people" behave, don't be that kind of rich person. Don't participate in the extractive capitalism that is killing our planet. Don't be the person who takes without considering the costs. You *always* have a choice about how to show up. Nothing—especially not money—can take that away from you.

But *never* give up your seat at the table. Instead, take your place among the heavy-hitters and become an example of something better.

THE ART OF THE EXCHANGE

Before you can start moving through the Circles of Contribution, you need to turn on the tap—aka, your money flow.

Yes, it's time to get people to pay you.

This is a huge hurdle for many people, whether they're solopreneurs, in the nonprofit space, or working within a company.

The biggest narrative I see among my clients is this: "By valuing myself and my services, I am 'taking' from people." This narrative shows up across multiple levels of business and income, and it couldn't be more untrue.

First of all, getting paid is the outward expression of owning your value. You're not Robin Hood, taking from the rich to give to the poor. In fact, you're not "taking" at all. The money you receive in exchange for the problems you solve is a mere fraction of the long-term value you are providing.

Second, you're giving money far too much weight. Money was invented to solve the logistical problems of barter. It's not a measure of your worth as a human, or your intellect, or your capacity to create impact. But it does happen to weigh less than goats.

Once upon a time, I would bring my three goats to market in town. If you were selling salt, we would figure out together how much of your salt was a fair trade for my goats. Once we agreed, you would take the goats, and I would take the salt, and we would both feel like we got something we needed.

Imagine if you said, "Oh, but my salt is just ... salt. It isn't really worth your goats. I wouldn't feel right about taking them. Maybe ... just one goat?"

Well, now I have a problem, because none of the fresh goat meat I have at home is getting preserved for the winter without your salt. This thing you have in abundance (and are actively trying to diminish) is actually vital to me and my well-being.

As a client, I *need* salt to thrive. In fact, I'm not leaving this market without salt. Now, I can either take your salt without giving you the goats—in which case, your family goes hungry as they work to harvest more undervalued salt for tomorrow, and I go home wondering if there is something inferior about this salt (because why else would you be giving it away for practically nothing?)—or, I find another salt-seller who owns the value of their product, and trade my goats to them.

When you look at it this way, refusing to own your value seems silly. No one wins, and it doesn't move anyone forward.

Today, things feel far more complicated than goats and salt—but in essence, nothing has changed. When you own your value and are willing to receive in a way that supports you and those you serve, value is created *on both sides*.

In fact, if you're operating from the powerful combination of wealth and impact consciousness, the other person will receive value *exponentially greater* than what you are accepting in exchange. After all, to you it's just salt—but to the guy with the goats, it's literally the difference between surviving and thriving.

The key to mastering this dynamic is something I call the Inner Sale. If you haven't sold yourself on your inherent value as a human and the miracle of your existence, and also on the true value of what you are providing to your clients and customers in the marketplace, you will always be paddling upriver against the flow of money. You can transcend any barriers to your Inner Sale through NLP (NeuroLinguistic Programming), therapy, coaching, energy work, meditation, or any other modality that calls to you—but in the end, owning your value is a *powerful decision*, and once you make it, there's no going back.

Once you have mastered the Inner Sale, people will feel your confidence, certainty, and clarity about your mission, vision, and purpose. You will confidently live out your Soul Mission and your clients, supporters, and stakeholders will be drawn to you more than ever before.

Your salt matters, my friend. Start acting like it.

6 | THE VELOCITY OF CAPITAL

"WHAT ABOUT A STOP in Detroit?" I asked my friend, who was carpooling with me from the East Coast to my parents' home in Chicago.

I was twenty-two years old, in my senior year of university. In pursuit of my American Studies degree (which, if you remember, was my new path of study after I veered away from investment banking), I had spent a lot of time studying population flow over the course of American history, as well as economics from a cultural perspective.

I wanted to see Detroit because it was used as an example in so many of my courses. My professors talked about the decline of the auto industry, the migration of former slaves from the emancipated South after the Civil War, the "white flight" of the 1970s and 1980s, and the effects of all these factors on the city and its population. It was a half-day detour from our planned route, but my friend agreed that it would be interesting to see the former stronghold of the auto barons.

Driving through the city in my friend's blue pickup truck, my mind was blown. It wasn't just the poverty—I'd seen plenty of that in West Philly, and worse in India. It was the sheer depth of the fall the city had taken. There were entire neighborhoods of lush mansions simply abandoned and left to rot. Multiple fast-food joints shared tiny retail spaces, protected on all sides by bulletproof glass. The train station, which must once have been reminiscent of Philadelphia's iconic 30th Street Station, was a nightmare of graffiti and shattered glass. As we passed through downtown during the lunch hour, I saw one lone dude in a suit; otherwise, the streets were empty.

How could such a thing have happened?

We parked at an abandoned factory and climbed through the gaping hole in the fence. Inside, there were still enormous pieces of equipment lying about, as well as evidence of squatters. I could feel that old prosperity like a ghost in the corners, grieving.

Driving out of the city that afternoon, I tried to digest what I'd seen. It was heartbreaking and weird and totally unlike anything I'd ever been exposed to. The only thing I understood in that moment was that money used to flow in Detroit, and now it didn't.

I wonder what you'd need to do to get money back into this place? I asked myself.

Money is the lifeblood of communities. If the money came back to Detroit, the city would come back to life. It was like a plant that wasn't being watered. I knew, of course, that it wasn't that simple—but maybe it could be. Maybe all the factors that made Detroit a place to escape from could be mitigated, if not reversed, by flows of money, and the jobs, services, and opportunities that the money river brings along with it.

If you want to change circumstances, no matter what they are, you must increase the velocity of capital moving through those circumstances. If a community, society, idea, or problem does not have at least one person who is skilled in the science of increasing the velocity of capital, change will be slow and painful, and will certainly never reach its maximum potential. Add just one person who can move money flows with skill, however, and everything changes.

We discussed some examples of impact-makers earlier

in this book, and how they moved money to create results. Now, think of some modern examples—like Scott Harrison, founder of Charity:Water, who used his skill at moving capital as a nightclub promoter to revolutionize how water is delivered to communities in Africa.

Once you work your way through the Circles of Contribution and are ready to start moving money in your community and around the globe, you will need to understand how to leverage the velocity of capital to maximize the impact your dollars (euros, pounds, yen, renminbi, rupees, etc.) can make.

This is the first step in building your Impact Empire.

THE MULTIPLIER EFFECT

In college, I studied economics in the context of social dynamics. One of the core concepts that has stayed with me since that time is something called the Multiplier Effect.

The Multiplier Effect is the proportional amount of increase (or decrease) in final income that results from an injection or withdrawal of funds. Certain activities and investments will "multiply" my dollar by a factor of two, or seven, or fifteen. Others will "dilute" my dollar so it comes back to me weaker than it started.

This was fascinating to me, especially in the context of gross domestic product (GDP). For example, one dollar invested in education leads to more than seven dollars in GDP growth. And, the faster a dollar "circulates" inside an economy, the stronger that economy becomes. We can see this in action in wealthy neighborhoods: injections of money through taxes produce the best schools, better property values, public health, etc. The faster that money moves inside an area—the more "velocity" each dollar has—the more money is attracted there. But in places where the money is withdrawn, the velocity of capital drops, and the result is a sharp downward spiral that sucks people—and impact potential—right down with it.

I saw this negative velocity in Detroit. I saw it in West Philly, where we lived for much of my childhood. I saw it starkly in India, and in South America, and many of the other places I visited as a young adult. As a social impact entrepreneur, I could go on all day about what's wrong with the above picture, and how we need to change it—but the fact remains, the Multiplier Effect is a real thing, and it produces real results *in both directions.* So, it's our job to harness this and other "natural laws" of money, and move our capital through the people, things, and ideas that create more good in the world.

When you use the Circles of Contribution to position yourself for impact, you tap into the power of the Multiplier Effect. You become the generator, the engine, that produces impact acceleration. Your money will create movement for your family, your employees, your community—and, when you're ready, the planet.

I want you to think about that for a moment. What if the velocity of the money *you* create could literally breathe life back into a community?

The incredible thing is, you can do this *without* participating in extractive capitalism, outdated income models, or sleazy sales tactics. You can solve the problem you identified in Chapter 4 without doing damage first and then trying to make it up through philanthropy. This may involve making different choices about your products, services, and distribution models—but it's possible. You can adhere to your highest standards and ideals and still produce a great product. You can have a positive impact on both sides of the equation.

THE INFINITY LOOP

So much of the cultural narrative about "asshole rich people" comes from the way businesses have been (and, in many cases, still are) structured. From the time of feudalism, the rich have relied on the labor of the poor to make them richer. Companies have exploited labor forces, natural resources, and whole communities to make their profits. They leveraged the velocity of capital but *gave that capital no outlet back into the community*. Some of these old-school capitalists did turn around and make massive monetary contributions—think Rockefeller, Carnegie, and others like them—but building a library or a university building can't undo decades of harm.

Here's the thing, my friend.

We don't have to do it their way.

I see money moving through each of us along a pathway I call The Infinity Loop.

The Infinity Loop

1	2	3	4	5
YOU	**WORK**	**CASH**	**GIVING**	**IMPACT**
giving & receiving for impact	solving a problem through service	getting paid for your services & solutions	flowing money into your circles of contribution	reaching your MIP, satisfaction, fulfillment

We are in the center, holding space for money to flow through us. On one side is our business or offering—the problem that we solve in the world. As we do our inspired work (in alignment with our values and principles, without exploitation of those who work for us), we impact others in a positive way, and they give us money in exchange. This money flows back to and through us at the center point.

Then, we get to send that money—that capital—into the other half of the Infinity Loop, where it can move through the causes, people, and ideas that matter to us, our community, and the planet. What comes back to us is joy, purpose, energy, sustenance—and yes, even money! With this level of return, we are powered up to keep doing our revenue-producing work (which, in itself, is impact-producing) and keep the cycle going. Meanwhile, the loop gets larger as our ability to hold the space expands. Soon, our Infinity Loop is touching people and ideas around the world—and nourishing us and our families the entire time.

As we've discussed, money is energy. When you stand at the center of that infinity loop, you are a conduit for impact energy. You are giving and receiving in proportion—and in total alignment with your ideals.

It used to be that you could either be a broke idealist or a rich jerk. But a tidal wave of new thinkers (like us) are proving that we can be both highly principled *and* incredibly wealthy. We can help others and ourselves at the same time. We can come to the money river with a boat big enough for everyone who wants to come along.

The key to creating your Infinity Loop is to remember that both sides of the equation need to be positioned for impact. We can no longer make money the old-fashioned, destructive way on one side and then do good works on the other. When we allow that, we are actually canceling out our Maximum Impact Potential. Donating 5 percent of your profits to a humanitarian charity doesn't mean shit if your manufacturing process uses child labor.

The problem you solve, which you identified in Chapter 4, can absolutely be solved without compromising your values and ideals. You might have to disrupt your entire industry to do it—like what I participated in when I was at the helm of Fed by Threads—but it is possible if you are willing to get creative in your approach.

Once you have the Infinity Loop in place, it's just a question of, "How good can I make this? How rapidly can I make those dollars move through this loop system?"

THE DICHOTOMY OF IMPACT

By now, you may have started to perceive a stark contrast between what we are talking about in this book—Maximum Impact Potential, the Infinity Loop, and Wealth Circulation—and what is happening "out there" in the world.

The truth is, there is a dark side to impact—just as there is a dark side to almost anything great on this planet. This dichotomy of light and dark is present in leadership, government, nonprofits, the corporate space ... pretty much anywhere humans exist. And so, it would be naïve not to assume that this dichotomy can—and does—show up in the impact space as well.

Money can be used for good or for evil; how we use it doesn't change its nature. Impact, likewise, can be positive or negative. The Infinity Loop can feed conscious, uplifting energy through a human ecosystem—or it can flow toxicity. As always, the deciding factor in this equation is *you.*

I could share plenty of examples of companies and people who harness the Infinity Loop for self-serving gain—who, instead of flowing funds outward from impact on the left side, reverse the flow to pull in capital through manipulation, unscrupulous marketing, and manufactured need, and then use those profits to feed the ravenous maw of their own organization, shareholders, and corporate interests. But the fact is, you already know that this "impact reversal" is happening. Maybe your unwillingness to feed the beast was what drew you toward the impact space in the first place.

Continually expanding your MIP in the direction of positivity, inclusivity, equity, planetary responsibility, and elevated consciousness takes one thing: *awareness.* As I shared at the start of this book, every decision you make, large or small, has the potential to elevate or reverse your

MIP. Now that you have the model of the Infinity Loop and a greater understanding of how money and energy cycle through you to create impact, you will also start to see how decisions made at different points on the Infinity Loop can affect the entire flow.

THE BIG PICTURE

Even when we know our mission, work, impact, and Circles of Contribution are aligned, we can sometimes feel like our ideals and values are in conflict with our desire for impact. We ask, "Am I thinking too big? Isn't it enough to have an impact at a personal level, and be content with that?"

Of course it is! However, there's a difference between deliberately expressing your MIP at a granular, one-to-one level and getting tunnel vision. Since you picked up this book, I think you know the difference already. You know you're being called to *more*. But if for any reason you're tempted to stop your expansion at Circle of Contribution #2 and call it a day, I want you to consider not what your expansion will mean for you, but what your playing small will mean for those who desperately need what you are creating.

I recently had a client who experienced a massive wakeup around his Maximum Impact Potential . Brian is a healing practitioner focused on helping high-powered men lead more balanced and loving lives, and he's doing great for himself. Over the course of the year he coached with me, I helped him double his practice, streamline his existing offers and systems, and hone in on his ideal client—aka, the person he most wanted to solve problems for. He never moved into the high-ticket, impact-focused space we had designed together—but, overall, anyone would have called our collaboration a huge success.

Anyone but me, I suppose.

On our final video call, we had a really honest conversation. "I have to tell you, man," I said. "I feel like a lot of our time was spent spinning wheels. You expanded a lot, but I feel like we never tapped into the magnitude of what's possible for you. I wasn't sensing that drive from you."

I could tell Brian was taken aback, but he said, "Be honest with me. Don't sugar coat it. How does my performance compare to that of your other clients?"

"Based on where you started, you underachieved. In fact, you achieved *less* than any of my other private clients. On paper, you're a top-one-percenter and went from $300,000 a year to $500,000 a year, but you didn't *really* go for it. And I'm wondering why. I have people with half your qualification, half your capability, half your capacity ... and they're going to fucking *lap* you in terms of both money and impact growth. They will outearn you, and they will touch way more lives doing it."

Brian sighed. "To be honest, I just don't have that burning desire. I'm happy. I have nothing to prove. The only thing I want is to be a wonderful dad to my little girl. She is my greatest achievement."

I understood exactly where he was coming from—and he was right. When his little girl walked into the room during our calls, he lit up like a Christmas tree. He was utterly devoted to her, and he had achieved a pretty remarkable balance between work and life in the pursuit of supporting her fully at every stage of her growth.

So why did I still feel like I had failed him?

As we sat there in silence, Brian's eyes welled up. Because he's usually so calm and emotionally centered, I knew something big was shifting inside him. "What's going on?" I asked.

"I just realized that, yeah, my daughter has a great dad—but what about all those other daughters? What about all the time they will lose with their own dads if I don't step up and talk about this?"

Now, we were both crying. I could feel the pain of all those other little girls who didn't get to have a wonderful dad like my client. "You don't need to change a thing, man. You don't need to step up. You don't *need* to do anything. Your daughter will have a great life, and she will be *so* loved, and that might be enough. But you have the capacity to serve in a bigger way—for those other daughters. *Will you do it?*"

"I will," he said. "Now that I've seen it, I have to."

It's your turn, reader.

Let me ask you now: *Will you do it?*

Will you become the kind of person who can hold space for that next level of service and impact?

Will you do what it takes to shift your focus and your narrative to something bigger than your inner circle?

Will you feel the pain and the scope and the immensity of the problem you're being called to solve—and face it head-on? Will you be the solution, instead of trying to stand outside the problem?

Will you learn how to move money flows through your ideas so you can bring life back into the people, places, and ideas that you care about?

And will you stand at the center of that Infinity Loop, holding space for change that is greater than anything you had ever envisioned before?

That's what my client is on track for now. And someday, little girls everywhere are going to have better lives because he helped to bring their happy, loving dads back.

If not you, then who?

7 | THE QUANTUM FACTOR

"HOLY CRAP!" I SHOUTED. "That's *it!*"

I was watching one of my favorite movies of all time, *The Matrix*, and had just gotten to the scene where Neo, staring down a black military helicopter, asks Trinity, "Can you fly that thing?"

Trinity responds, "Not yet," and proceeds to request a pilot program for a B-212 helicopter.

In an instant, knowledge about how to fly a military

copter is downloaded into her brain, and she is ready to execute the task within the simulation.

It was as if the Universe had plucked me out of my seat and dropped me in a whole new reality. Hello, red pill.

I'd been struggling to understand how some people could create exponential results in their impact spaces, while others who were doing *all the same things* simply kept trudging along, logging incremental growth but never gaining momentum. I wanted to create a tool for my clients to use that would invite radical expansion in a predictable way. Now, suddenly, all the various pieces came together: The Law of Attraction and mindset hacks I'd been learning from my coaches, the success habits I'd been reading about for decades, the very real data being gathered by scientists about the nature of the Universe ... and Trinity's helicopter.

The truth is, we have access to all the information, courage, perspective, and vision we need to take the next steps toward our Maximum Impact Potential, because *the version of us who has accomplished all of these things already exists as a possibility in the quantum field and is therefore accessible to us at any time.* I saw how I could exponentially accelerate my own impact potential, and help my clients accelerate theirs, simply by stepping into the version of me who had already been there, done that, and lived to tell the tale.

I won't lie, it was an awesome moment. There may have been a loud *whoop-whoop* and a few air-punches involved.

IMPACT BOTTLENECKS

Earlier in this book, I asked you to accept and embrace the fact that your potential is equivalent to that of all the impact giants you admire—to take your seat at the table, and recognize that your contribution can be just as significant if you choose to engage your MIP. That was the first step, but to put everything you've learned in this book into action, you will need to take it even further. It's time to fully own your *perception of* and *contribution to* your current reality, and your power to shape your future.

You see, now that you have the basis of your MIP established—owning your value, choosing your work path, your current Circle of Contribution, and your Infinity Loop—you will begin to put all this knowledge to work in real time. When you do, I guarantee you will run into one or more of what I call "Impact Bottlenecks." These bottlenecks have nothing to do with your company, your niche, or your impact pathway, but *everything* to do with how you perceive and engage with your reality.

The Five Most Common Impact Bottlenecks

1. Not being deliberate about your state of being
2. Not accepting the integrated nature of wealth and impact (aka, money mindset)
3. Not trusting yourself, others, or the Universe

4. Not asking for help

5. Not shifting your negative emotional states

Yes, I'm phrasing these bottlenecks in the negative. Why? Because, as with everything else related to your MIP, these bottlenecks aren't "blocks," or "obstacles." Not being deliberate, not accepting, not trusting, not asking for help, not adjusting your outlook ... those are *decisions*.

At every stage of the game, at every level of your Maximum Impact Potential, at every crossroads moment, you can choose to do the thing, or not do the thing. That's not to say that there won't be a massive learning curve on the other side of your choice. But the choice itself is clear-cut: open up the impact fire hose, or crimp the flow.

Let's break these Bottlenecks down one by one.

IMPACT BOTTLENECK #1: NOT BEING DELIBERATE ABOUT YOUR STATE OF BEING

The state of being that we occupy is based on our perception of reality. Everything we understand as "truth" is really just a perspective defined by information we have accumulated and stored away in our brains through experience, social conditioning, and observation.

Most people look at the evidence in their current reality and allow that to influence and define their state of being. They say, "This is the level of impact I'm making," or "This is my current circle of contribution," and they make decisions from that level of reality.

However, there is no better way to crimp your impact fire hose than to act from your circumstances and the current version of yourself.

The truth is, there are *multiple versions* of you that exist right now. Among them are your current self, your more-successful (and more-impactful) self, and your less-successful (and less-impactful) self. The quantum field is energy and possibility. Every choice we make moves us closer to, or further from, a set of possibilities—but no matter what we choose, the possibilities are *still there*. This is why, no matter what we've done in the past, we always have the potential to increase our Maximum Impact Potential in this lifetime.

Many people don't believe that being who they are being right now is a choice. But I can promise you: the people who are achieving the most impact, most quickly, are not doing so from the current version of themselves. They're not waiting for their current reality to validate their decisions, or show them the way forward. Instead, they're tapping into the version of them who has already achieved it all. Just like happiness, impact and success are *choices*. They have to happen within you before they can happen outside of you.

The version of you who is living your MIP is already present for you in the quantum field and in your subconscious mind. That version of you—that set of possibilities—functions like an inner divining rod. When you want to step into that iteration of you, all you have to do is ask, "What would my future self say to me right now?" You will almost always have the answer. It's right there, in the space between heartbeats.

If you don't believe me, ask yourself, "How easy is it for me to slip into my *less* successful, *less* impactful self?" You know, the version of you who worries, doubts, plays the victim, procrastinates, self-sabotages? The version of you who failed, and who has all the evidence to prove you will fail again? I'll bet *that* self is totally present for you at the snap of your fingers. Admit it, it's easier to see that version of you, since maybe you've already been there. But that version of you is *no more or less real* than the future, more successful version of you. The mindset shift is exactly the same, and requires the same amount of effort. You've simply made a choice to pay this past, less-successful version more attention.

Stepping into your Maximum Impact Potential requires you to embrace a version of you whom you haven't yet come to know—the version of you who has the courage to go to that event, or leave the crappy job, or hire the right people. The unknown can be scary—but in the end, the future you is still *you*. It's just a matter of perception.

So, as you consider how best to put what you've learned in this book to work, let me ask you: Are you courageous enough to step into a version of you who you haven't met yet—a version of you who is doing the things you want to do and making the impact you want to make? Are you ready to take a leap of faith, and recognize that you have the power to decide which version of you to be, every single day?

Once again, you're at a moment of choice. You can decide this whole section is a crock of shit ... or you can take it for a test drive, and decide to operate as the most successful, impactful, aligned version of you for the next three, six, or twelve months. What's the risk? It's free, it's easy, and it takes place entirely in your own head. It's literally the most accessible evolutionary tool at your disposal.

I promise: when you climb into that future version of you—the version who has already done and experienced all the things you're dreaming about—the Universe will recalibrate around you, and start presenting you all the evidence you could ever need. Only, you won't need it anymore, because you will already be connecting with the next future version of you.

And if you choose not to do this? You'll keep moving forward. But you'll be limited to the possibilities available to you as you are today, not as you will be tomorrow.

IMPACT BOTTLENECK #2: NOT ACCEPTING THE INTEGRATED NATURE OF WEALTH AND IMPACT

Given what we've learned throughout this book, you'd think this one would be simple ... and yet, so many people I coach struggle with this bottleneck.

A lot of people will call this work "money mindset." I call it Wealth Consciousness.

A better relationship with money starts with owning your value, which we covered in Chapter 3. The next step—the one that so often trips up impact creators—is to release the relationship between impact and effort.

Your life force energy is capital, just like money. Only, unlike money, it isn't infinite. You only have a certain amount of life force energy to spend, and only a certain number of hours in your day. And if you want to maximize your MIP over the course of a lifetime, you have to recognize that creating more money flow and becoming a wealth circulator does not equal working yourself into the ground. When you grind something over and over, it eventually turns to dust.

No one benefits when we burn out. And yet, I see people doing it to themselves all the time when they decide to create more money flows in their business or mission space. They become workaholics, and make unhealthy sacrifices around their health, relationships, or joy in service to their mission. Furthermore, they become the bottleneck in their wealth circulation, because their mentality around money and hard work prevents them from receiving with ease within the Infinity Loop.

I used to be a total workaholic. Some would still put me

in that category, because I love my work, and I work a lot. But over the years, I've learned to pace myself. I know now that my money flows are not correspondent to the number of hours I put in, but rather to the quantum capacity I create within myself to be a channel for money, and to the team I surround myself with. If I want to continue to scale my impact for the next thirty, forty, or fifty years, I *can't* burn myself out. Nor am I willing to sacrifice my closest relationships on the altar of my impact.

If you bring a "hustle and grind" mentality into your impact work (regardless of your industry), you will have an above-average impact in the short term, but you'll set yourself on a collision course for burnout. It's the same concept as giving away all of your oranges. When there's nothing left—when you collapse from exhaustion, illness, or the sheer emotional weight of the hustle—you won't even be able to take care of yourself, let alone facilitate impact for anyone else.

The solution to this bottleneck is to make better choices around how you relate to money. Step into that future version of you—the version who is a wealth circulator occupying the Circle of Contribution you aspire to inhabit—and operate from that place. That version of you knows that the level at which you receive money has nothing to do with how "hard" you work, and everything to do with your ability to attract and circulate capital. Once you flip that internal switch, you will open up the spigot and allow money to move freely through you and your cause.

IMPACT BOTTLENECK #3: NOT TRUSTING YOURSELF, OTHERS, OR THE UNIVERSE

Those of us who are drawn to the impact space tend to share several qualities. We're openhearted. We love people and the planet. We care about doing good things in the world. We are aware of how our actions, big and small, can make a difference.

And, we're naturally trusting. Sometimes *too* trusting. We get taken advantage of. We get hurt when we innocently trust people and institutions that are not aligned with our impact vision—and, over the course of a lifetime, accumulate a mountain of evidence that others are untrustworthy. Worse, we start believing that we can't trust ourselves or our decisions.

My story around trust was challenging for a long time. I had a belief from my days at Fed By Threads and in other businesses that I didn't hire well. I chose people because I wanted to teach and uplift them, not because they were perfect for the job. Over and over, I was left to carry the weight of the business on my own shoulders after people let me down. I wondered, "Is there *anyone* out there who can do what I do, as well as I do it?"

This double lack of trust—in my own ability to hire well, and in others' ability to do their jobs well—created a huge roadblock in my business and my MIP. When I created my coaching business, I didn't want to hire at all. I figured I'd just go it alone. But within two years, I hit an "impact ceiling": a place where my growth (both financial and impact) was literally stopped dead because I physically could not do any more than I was doing.

I was forced to make a choice: Would I trust, and potentially fail again after I worked so hard to get where I was? Or would I accept that I had hit my growth ceiling, and could no longer do better, dream bigger, or expand beyond my own current reach?

It hardly seems like a choice at all, put that way. But it *was* a choice, and a difficult one.

In the end, I chose trust.

I also made the choice to hire as my future self—the version of me who already had the thriving impact business, the kick-ass team, and the ability to delegate wisely. I called in a team of A-players who could actually help me execute my biggest vision. I hired with my head as well as my heart. And I chose to trust—fully trust—that my new team could do the work as well or better than I could do it alone.

The result? Unlimited impact potential. Unlimited upside. Unlimited flow through that Infinity Loop. It's really amazing.

If you're having trust issues in your impact space—whether it's around team, colleagues, donors, or something else entirely—I would encourage you to ask three simple questions: "Do I trust myself? Do I trust other people? Do I trust the Universe?"

If the answer is no (on any front), you have a choice. You can continue to operate from your current state of being. Or, you can step into the future, more impactful version of you, and start making decisions from there. Chances are, the future version of you knows all about trust, and what kinds of miracles can be worked when trust energy is in play. It might feel a bit like "Fake it till you make it," but really, it's more like, "Wear the clothes until you grow into them."

As we learned in Chapter 4 , you have the choice to see the world as working *for* you or working *against* you. When you choose to trust, you also accept that the world is a beautiful place, and that you, as a speck of awesomeness, have the potential to be more than just a blip in the historical record.

IMPACT BOTTLENECK #4: NOT ASKING FOR HELP

One of my big "a-ha" moments after my epic low point in 2016 was that, throughout my whole career as a leader, I had never asked for help. You could make a generalization that I am just another hardheaded man (and that might be partially true) but it was more complex than that.

There were actually two devastating forces at play: ego and embarrassment.

I was taught that entrepreneurs are "problem solvers" and "independent thinkers." I translated that to mean, "they figure things out on their own, always have their shit together, and never show weakness." This wasn't (and isn't) true, obviously, but that was my belief, which led to embarrassment because I didn't always have solutions to what was happening in my work arena. I thought something was wrong with me. I watched with envy as others "cracked the code" faster than me, and skyrocketed to success.

This combination of ego and embarrassment was brutal, and the result was that I constantly scrambled to cover it up when I didn't know what I was doing, duct tape it all together, and pray that somehow, with enough hard work on my part, everything would magically fall into place. When my ideas succeeded, I reasoned, I could breathe again. No one would know that I was winging it the whole time.

You already know how well *that* worked out. It was utter stupidity—and yet, I persisted.

In my defense, I literally had no idea that coaching was a thing. Coaches and mentors were mentioned in the books I was devouring, but it never occurred to me that other CEOs in my network had people behind the scenes to give them perspective when things got rough, or to help them expand their visions. I was blind to the fact that no one can do this work alone—and that none of the most successful people even *try* to do it alone!

I also spent a ton of energy on jealousy, envy, and anger. I was seeing so many people in my arena getting great results, and yet I was barely moving forward. All the YouTube videos, books, and podcasts in the world couldn't shift the block that was my ego.

When I got that first customer service job—and later, when I was selling for other industry leaders—I saw how coaching literally transformed people's lives and businesses. I saw people getting customized solutions and emotional support, not just information. And I saw the fatal flaw that had strangled my own impact for so many years: my insistence on doing it alone.

I don't know how I missed it for so long! Steve Jobs had a coach. Michael Jordan had many types of coaches. Tony Robbins has a whole team of coaches. Why wouldn't I do the same?

Today, I coach hundreds of movement-makers in the entrepreneurial space to position and scale their impact businesses. I also consult for more traditional businesses around how to bring the concept of MIP, the velocity of capital, and the Infinity Loop into their leadership vision. And, at the same time, I hire coaches for my own growth. I'm in high-level masterminds with people who are doing what I'm doing and *doing it better than me.* I still devour books on sales, leadership, and personal growth—but when I'm stuck, I never try to solve the issue on my own. Instead, I go directly to the people who have been there, done that, and left a trail of impact for me to follow.

True high achievers value time over money, and outcomes over ego. They will do whatever it takes to implement new ideas, actions, and ways of being *faster* so they can create powerful results. That's why they're willing to invest at high levels to work with those who can accelerate their progress.

Asking for help requires a tremendous level of vulnerability. We need to acknowledge that we can't, in fact, power through on will alone. Sometimes, we need to recalibrate our definition of "entrepreneurship" or "leadership," as I did. Sometimes, we need to be brave enough to air our shortcomings in a room full of other successful people in order to have the breakthrough we're seeking. And sometimes, we have to be willing to change the ways we have defined ourselves for our entire lives.

Hard-headed, stubborn, hustler, unicorn, renegade, rebel ... these are *MIP killers!* When you insist on being different than any other human out there, when you insist on forging your own path instead of listening to others who have actually done the things you want to do, you are essentially saying to God and the Universe, "I don't need any of the magic you have. I don't need universal wisdom. I don't need other humans, or the accumulated wisdom of centuries. I do it my own way."

I hope you can see how idiotic that is.

The more you become an expert in your impact niche, the more you *need* to practice Beginner's Mind.

I'm now considered an expert in aligned sales, coaching, and social impact entrepreneurship. In terms of wealth circulation and annual sales, I'm in the top 1 percent of coaches in the world. And yet, I make it my goal to come to every training with Beginner's Mind, as if I know nothing. Because I understand that, if I am open, there is a possibility that I will receive a single gem that will change the trajectory of my work, and my MIP, forever. This is not to say that I blindly accept everything I learn in my masterminds, coaching groups, or trainings—only that I am willing to *not know* so that I can learn to be better.

So, if you're not asking for help around your business and impact potential, and you're not getting the results you know are possible, it's time to re-frame, swallow your pride, and raise your fucking hand.

IMPACT BOTTLENECK #5: NOT SHIFTING YOUR NEGATIVE EMOTIONAL STATES

Anger, fear, frustration, jealousy, sadness, hatred, envy ... these emotions instantly repel everything that you desire.

Let that land for a moment.

Don't misunderstand me: there's nothing wrong with *feeling* these things. They are part of our human emotional spectrum, and they are useful tools for helping us see where we aren't acting in purpose, alignment, and integrity. But *staying* in those states for long periods of time—not allowing those emotions to move through you and be learned from and integrated—will absolutely destroy your MIP.

On the other hand, "power emotions" attract opportunity and impact potential. Enthusiasm, joy, gratitude, happiness, and celebration are magnetic. People and opportunities can't help but come toward you. Doors open. Magic unfolds.

So go the emotions in your body, so goes everything.

This is important to understand because so many social impact entrepreneurs I know are *absolutely fucking furious*. They're fighting the good fight, pushing back, challenging the system. They're going to war against injustice, inequity, and oppression. They're also miserable, cynical, and exhausted.

From a universal perspective, we can't create from a negative. Saying "I'm fighting poverty" is not the same as saying, "I am becoming a Wealth Circulator to create opportunities for others." The universe doesn't hear *can't*, *won't*, *don't*, or *not*. It simply hears, "I want poverty," because your energy is focused on poverty.

From an MIP perspective, the impact potential of someone in a negative state is exponentially less than that of someone in a positive one. Righteous anger is still anger—and anger blinds you to opportunity.

So, if you're carrying a daily load of anger, cynicism, hatred, envy, frustration, or any other challenging emotions, consider how you could flip those negative viewpoints and start inviting more "power emotions" into your life. Ask for help to process and transmute your feelings.

There is a simple methodology I give to all of my private clients. I call it the TREEE Process.

You can either be a rotted TREEE or a blossoming TREEE. When you're in a persistent negative state, you can use this process to make that shift.

The TREEE Process has five simple components:

1. *Trigger:* A thought, event, or experience.
2. *Response:* All the ways your mind reacts to the trigger.
3. *Emotion:* The feelings that start to swirl in your body in reaction to your Response.
4. *Effort:* What action (or lack thereof) do your Response and Emotion provoke?
5. *Effect:* What is the result of the Effort you expended (or didn't) following your Response and Emotion?

Sometimes, we don't have control over our triggers. Stuff happens in life, and we need to deal with it. Even our thoughts aren't fully conscious. But the Trigger isn't where most people go off-track. That happens in the Response phase.

Take these two side-by-side examples.

	Rotted TREEE	Blossoming TREEE
Trigger	"I want to create a super successful, multi-million-dollar impact-driven business so I can fully live into my MIP."	"I want to create a super successful, multi-million-dollar impact-driven business so I can fully live into my MIP."
Response	"Who do you think you are? You can't do that. You've failed every time you've tried, and let everyone down. Just stick to what you know."	"I am fully supported by the Universe. So, what version of me do I need to become to accomplish that? Who do I need to surround myself with?"
Emotion	Frustration, anger, disappointment, shame, apathy	Excitement, curiosity, anticipation, confidence, clarity, purpose
Effort	Busy work, avoidance, or nothing at all	Focused, inspired, targeted
Effect	Nothing changes	Progress is made

In both examples, the Trigger is the same. But things change at the Response level, when a person creates negative, limiting beliefs in response to the Trigger. This causes negative emotion to swirl in their body, which in turn prompts them to lose hope and stay stuck. This immediately plateaus, or even plummets, our business and impact.

Remember, nothing in the Universe stays in neutral. Everything in nature is either in expansion/growth toward its fullest expression, or in contraction/decline toward death. We are no exception—but when it comes to our own creations, work, and impact, we have a choice about which energy prevails.

The mistake most people make is that they try to heal the TREEE in the Effort phase. They push through the challenging feelings instead of resolving them. This only leads to more frustration because they are trying to work against negative thought and feelings. It's hugely draining, and in the long term, unsustainable.

A blossoming TREEE begins with your beliefs. Remember when, earlier in this book, we talked about being specks of awesomeness? Remember how we discovered that your Maximum Impact Potential is equal to that of anyone you revere? You can choose to put that knowledge to work here. Say the words in the Blossoming TREEE column to yourself, aloud. Can you feel the shift in your energy just by saying and thinking them? Catch your Responses when they happen, and you will change your trajectory forever.

Now, I know that this is easy to say. It's much less easy to do. While the derailment happens at the Response level, most of us aren't that aware of our own thoughts. We're much more likely to catch things at the Emotion level. When you start feeling emotions like anger, fear, doubt, or worry, your body is telling you that your mind is running through some negative Responses. Emotions are like fire alarms: ignore them at your peril.

When you know that your emotions are triggered by Responses in your mind, you can go to work. Identify the Responses all the way back to the original Trigger. Was it a statement you made? An encounter with a friend? A success or challenge in your business? Once you have it, take a moment to create a new, powerful Response to the Trigger. This will create a cascade that leads to more empowering Emotions, Efforts, and Effects.

Using the TREEE Process takes some practice, but once you begin to use it regularly, you will be able to move yourself into powerful states of being at will.

ACTIVATING QUANTUM RESULTS

My client, Jenna Hedstrom, showed up in my mastermind ready to tackle everything that was standing in the way of her MIP. She busted through her bottlenecks, made huge internal shifts in a matter of weeks, started to own her value and connect to her MIP for the first time since starting her business.

She went from practically zero sales when she began

to generating $43,000 in a twelve day stretch just a couple months later. In total that month, she closed more than $56,000 in new deals in her impact-driven coaching and healing business, a truly remarkable result.

But before one of our last group calls, she messaged me saying "I might cry on today's call and just wanted to prepare you." I was caught off-guard by this comment; surely we would be celebrating her huge wins?

But Jenna wasn't feeling celebratory. After out-creating every limitation she had previously perceived in her business, and getting a level of results beyond her biggest dreams ... she'd woken up that morning to discover that her credit card processor had flagged her account. The massive abundance flowing toward her had triggered a full-scale fraud alert. Tens of thousands of dollars were being withheld from her accounts, pending investigation.

"Alok," she said, "You've taught me that I'm a powerful creator of my reality, and I'm racking my brain right now to try to uncover what about me is still sabotaging my success. Why am I still not able to receive this level of wealth? What's wrong with me?"

"Are you open to a different explanation?" I asked.

She nodded.

"You *are* a powerful creator of your reality. You stepped into your future self and literally bent time and space to become her. You created such quantum-level results that our three-dimensional reality couldn't catch up. You're so powerful that you *broke the system.*"

And, just like that, her energy shifted. She was able to resolve the payment issues within a few days. And, as she later reflected to me, as a coach who teaches women to create quantum shifts and become empowered creators of their own reality, it was fitting that she led the way.

Jenna did the work. She aligned with—and became—her most successful future self. She aligned her consciousness to accept that wealth and impact are inseparable. She trusted herself, the Universe, and the people around her. She asked for help when she needed it. She moved through her frustration and fear so she could put her energy into empowered emotions.

Most of all, she made her commitment to her mission bigger than any of the bottlenecks she encountered. She chose to have something different, something *more.* She made a powerful decision to be an impact creator, a wealth circulator, and a force for healing in the world.

You are only a choice away from doing the same.

PART III

UPLIFT MILLIONS

8 YOUR IMPACT EMPIRE

I'LL NEVER FORGET the moment I saw my "impact ripple" clearly for the first time.

I was on a call with my client, Sanyika "The Firestarter" Street, creator of the All-In Method, and we were working through his impact plan—to help 100 men become millionaires, "go all in" in their lives and work, and become who they were born to be.

As we spoke that day, a huge energetic shift took place—

a shift that changed how I saw my own impact, and that of my clients, forever.

As Sanyika spoke that day, I could literally *see* our connection like a matrix of Universal energy. I saw him uplifting the lives of those 100 men, helping them change their financial realities and create their own Maximum Impact Potential. Each of those 100 men would then weave their own webs of impact, touching the lives of their families, friends, and clients through their own work. Then, all of those family, friends, and clients would continue to ripple the impact outward, into infinity.

The "footprint" of that impact was global.

My whole body lit up from the inside. I broke out in goosebumps. "Sanyika," I said. "Do you know that this work—your work with 100 men—will irrevocably change *a million lives*?"

I explained the matrix of impact I was seeing in my mind. As I did, I saw this truth take root within him. All at once, and for the first time, he saw his Maximum Impact Potential in the same way I saw it.

It was an emotional moment. I was thrilled beyond belief for the gifts that Sanyika is bringing to the world. And, because I was helping Sanyika step into his MIP and claim his power in the impact space, I knew that *I was a part of the matrix, too.*

YOUR MILLION PERSON IMPACT PLAN

How will *you* impact one million (or more) lives in your lifetime?

It may seem like a huge endeavor, but when you map it out, it becomes not only possible but well within your reach. I saw this impact matrix spreading out from Sanyika's work. By empowering his clients to be more powerful, vulnerable, motivated, and self-aware, he is also impacting the lives of his clients' partners, children, friends, colleagues, and employees. All of those human beings, in turn, will show up differently, impacting those around them. Even if you only walk this out to the third or fourth degree, the ripple is massive.

I see the same impact matrix in my own work, and the work of every one of my movement-maker clients. I see it for *you*.

Sometimes, "impact" can seem like a hazy space. We have trouble quantifying it. We know we want to create it—but it's only when you put actual numbers to it that it becomes *real*. You can actually quantify things like, "How many lives will be changed if 100,000 people read this book?" or, "How many lives will be changed if I serve 1,000 people through my nonprofit this year?" The numbers don't lie—and they add up quickly.

In this section, I'll show you how to quantify your impact and create your Million Person Impact Plan—a real strategy for impacting one million people through the various facets of your work.

I created this plan for my clients, most of whom are coaches, consultants, healers, influencers, and movement makers in the "knowledge economy" sector. However, you can just as easily apply this to your work through a product-driven business, a nonprofit, or as an employee within a traditional company. Just modify the category examples to fit your niche and impact vision.

CREATE YOUR MILLION PERSON IMPACT PLAN

1. In the middle of a large piece of paper, draw a circle. This is YOU.

2. Around the circle, create "branches" for all the various ways in which you want to deliver impact. Strategies my clients have used include:

    *   The products, services, or programs you offer through your business

    *   Masterminds, workshops, and retreats

    *   Personal relationships (including family, friends, and intimate partners)

    *   Social media and email marketing

    *   Podcasting and vlogging

    *   Participating in summits and live events

    *   Launching a product

- Volunteering, philanthropy, and donations

3. Estimate how many people you are already impacting in each of those spaces. Add those numbers to your paper. (First degree)

4. Estimate how many people around those first-degree people will be changed by the impact you're having. (Second degree)

5. Estimate how many people will be affected by the next ripple once the lives of the people in the second-degree group change. (Third degree)

6. Estimate the generational and community-wide impact when all of those people are positively affected (Fourth degree)

Here's an example of how this works in my company:

- ***Clients:*** Right now, I'm working with forty movement makers in my top-level mastermind, plus another hundred or so people in my other programs. I know that I can radically change their lives and businesses through the deep work we do. If those 140 people transform their relationships to business, impact, and money, they will in turn directly impact at least another 200 or more people, including their family, friends, and clients. Those 200 people will then go on to impact at least another 100 people each. (Note, these are super conservative estimates!) That's 2,800,000 people's lives changed for the better at the Third Degree level. Whoa.

- *Personal life:* What I'm doing in the impact space has a huge influence on my inner circle. This one is a bit harder to quantify, but I know that my son, Sequoia, will touch tens of thousands or even millions of people in his lifetime, no matter what career he chooses to pursue. That impact is part of my matrix, even if I can't fully quantify it yet. Same with my entire inner circle of friends and relatives. It's an enormous ripple.

- *Social media/platforms:* If I reach 10,000 social media followers this month, and each of them pass on something they've learned to 2 friends, and those two friends are positively impacted as well, and they influence 2 more friends, that's 120,000 people just this month—or 1,440,000 people a year.

- *Philanthropy:* As of the time of this writing, I donate funds to plant 10,000 trees a month through a charity that helps rural families create sustainable "food forests." Through donations, I also cure blindness for fifty people per month, and feed 10,000 meals to the homeless and hungry. These donations alone impact roughly 200,000 people a year.

- *Other:* I'm deeply dedicated to empowering women to reach financial sovereignty. I circulate wealth inside organizations like Kiva.org, which facilitate microlending to women in developing countries. The dollars I've put into those programs have circulated to more than a hundred women at the time of this writing. As each woman pays back her microloan, my donations become available to lend to another woman. As each woman creates success in her business, thousands of people—from her customers to her family and community—are positively affected. Eventually she employs people from her family and neighborhood, causing that wealth to begin to circulate in her community.

When you get real about the work you're doing and the impact it creates, you will see that every action you take *matters.* Even if you only have one client right now, or your nonprofit is in its infancy, or your company is just starting to implement an impact vision, you are making a difference.

Do this exercise for yourself; I promise, it will be totally eye-opening. No matter where you are in your impact journey, once you get to the third and fourth degree of impact, you'll start to see some serious numbers.

When you're done, pause for a moment and take in what you've just discovered.

You are at the center of this impact matrix.

You are the reason all these lives will be changed.

Your work is already making a difference *on a massive scale.*

Every choice you make from this day forward can take what you're already doing and expand it exponentially. Every new client you add, every contribution you make, every product you sell, every social media broadcast you do ... all of it ripples out around the planet in breathtaking ways.

Now, you may be tempted to say "But Alok, these numbers could be inflated. How do we know for sure ..."

Of course we don't know for sure. We likely never will. So, chop the numbers in half if you're skeptical. But then, multiply them by the remaining years of your life during which you plan to continue creating your MIP. I promise that, no matter how conservative you are in your estimates, you will see the vastness of your Impact Empire.

GETTING TO THE BIG NUMBERS

As you go through the process of creating your impact plan, I want you to keep a few things in mind.

First, you will want to know exactly how you desire to work in that first degree of impact. Do you want to go deep and create massive, sweeping change in the lives of a relative few, and let your impact be felt in the second, third, and fourth degrees as generational or community-wide change? Or do you want to impact a lot of people in a more surface-level way that casts a wide net of influence?

Clients tell me all the time, "I want to do deep work with a lot of people." I won't say that's impossible, but it's rare that someone can actually accomplish this. Think about your favorite influencers, event leaders, or business gurus—the ones with million-person audiences. Sure, they've given you great tidbits, and maybe even changed the direction of some aspect of your life. But have they helped you *fundamentally shift who you're being in the world*, at a deep level that will ripple through generations? I'd venture to say, probably not. Chances are, if you've had those kinds of results, it's been from a direct personal connection and deep work with an individual or small group.

There's nothing wrong with wanting to directly impact a huge segment of the population. Just recognize that you will approach this differently than you would a more intimate group. Your strategies will be different, as will your messaging. When you're serving a big audience, you will have more success by showing people small steps forward. It's the difference between feeding 10,000 people a single meal and helping ten people learn how to create economic opportunities that feed thousands for years to come. Both are equally valid, but one approach is focused on shifting things in the moment and moving the needle a little bit for a lot of people, while the other is focused on creating bigger change in the long term for a smaller group.

Second, if you aren't quite where you want to be in your impact zone, you also use this technique to reverse-engineer your impact plan. If, for example, you have a goal to impact one million lives, you can work the numbers backward to see *exactly* how many people you need to touch in each area of your life and business to realize your goal—and make a plan from there.

Third, remember that what we measure grows. If you want to scale your impact, start paying attention to the numbers, scope, and depth of what you're already doing. Don't act like your efforts don't matter, or like your donations are small potatoes. Feel the ripple you're creating through your impact matrix, measure it diligently, and make a plan to scale it.

BUILDING YOUR IMPACT EMPIRE

A lot of people cringe when I say the words "Impact Empire."

It's true that "empire" has had a negative association for a long time. From the time of the Ottoman and Roman empires to our modern era, the theme of empire was conquest. Empires were typically measured by their geographic footprint—the amount of land, resources, and people under their rule. Today, we are seeing corporate empires, where the "spoils" aren't about rivers and cities but market dominance and customer dollars.

I don't use the term empire lightly. I truly believe we are in the midst of a third evolution of the concept—one which is inclusive, equitable, and non-competitive. Instead of trying to "own" a space in the impact sector and slay the competition, I see movement makers like us starting to realize that transformation and impact aren't exclusive commodities— that our domain is measured in lives touched, and that those same lives can be impacted by many people and businesses over the course of a lifetime, all to the greater good.

I think of the range of our Impact Empire in terms of Human Geographic Footprint (HGF). What would it look like if you could put a pin on a globe for every person around the world who is impacted by your MIP? Can you imagine that impact footprint covering more and more of the planet as time goes on? That is your Impact Empire expanding. But unlike in the past, there are not border disputes: you and I can *both* impact the same person's life, whether they live in Nairobi or Chicago. This is the measure of our empire—and where empires overlap, the positive effect is multiplied, not diminished. It's borderless impact.

Much of your Human Geographic Footprint is made possible by technology. You can build a worldwide network with nothing but an internet connection and a smartphone, and start the ripple of your work with a single person in a single location. Emmanuel Ofosu Yeboah changed a nation because *someone gave him a bike*. Your work, too, can start breaking old paradigms and transforming generational stories across the world, one person at a time.

Your Impact Empire can also be hyper-local. Maybe you want to increase the velocity of capital in your community, and keep the money you funnel through your Infinity Loop in your hometown. Maybe you want to help a specific group of people in your city in a deep, meaningful way. This doesn't mean you are building less of an empire. It simply means your HGP is concentrated in a smaller geographical area. Your work can still end up spreading impact around the world!

For example, consider Slum Dwellers International. The charity began in Mumbai, in the district of Dharavi. Over a million people live there, in an area of just over two square kilometers. It's one of the largest slums in Asia, and one of the most impoverished places on Earth. At its founding, Slum Dwellers International focused on empowering people from Dharavi to improve access to basic services, change harsh eviction and police policies, and understand that a better way is possible. However, after the level of success the founders were able to create in Dharavi, the idea spread to other slum cities and poor urban areas. Today,

SDI is an international federation with representatives from India, Asia, Africa, and Latin America. They're helping to create an entire generation of urban poor who think differently about who they are, what's possible for them, and what they can contribute to society.

CIRCLES OF CONTRIBUTION AND IMPACT EMPIRE

You may be wondering where the Circles of Contribution fit in this discussion—and if it's possible to have a global impact if you're currently in Circle #1 or #2.

The answer is yes, but with a caveat.

You can begin to expand your Human Geographic Footprint no matter what your money flows are. You can work with clients, customers, or colleagues around the world, and create ripples of change through them, starting today. But where your personal capacity ends, *so does your impact.*

Money is the difference between impact at a granular level and impact on a huge scale. Human to human, you can create impact with less capital. With wealth moving through your vision, you can create a movement.

Let's come back to the example of Slum Dwellers International. Could that organization's founders have made a difference by simply *talking* to the residents of Dharavi, with no cash to back them up? Sure. But with money flowing through the organization—with the ability to provide resources as well as information—they can measurably shift circumstances and futures for *millions.*

In the coaching space, where I work, I see clients making a beautiful difference on a person-to-person level in their businesses while they are still in Circle #1. But when they have money flowing through their vision, they can reach more people. Hire teams. Become wealth circulators. Break generation cycles of poverty, oppression, and cultural shame. And, most importantly, feel 100 percent supported to do their work at the highest level without burning out. They evolve into CEOs of impact-driven companies living into their MIP.

My point is, your impact isn't negated if you don't have cash flow right now. (Doing your Impact Plan exercise will prove that!) But neither is it amplified. When you and your personal energy are the *only* thing powering your impact, you will never be able to build on it. You will never multiply it. You will never increase the size of your dominoes.

Where many of my clients get stuck is on the numbers. They know the difference they want to make, but don't understand why they need to get to a certain Circle to accomplish it. "What you're talking about seems like way more money than I need to do what I want to do," they'll say.

One client of mine told me that he wanted his teachings to reach a million people.

"How much do you think that costs?" I asked him.

He was taken aback. "I don't know. Maybe $100,000?"

"More like twenty times that. I mean, you *might* win the viral content lottery—but do you really want to bank your life's work on that?"

When we broke down the mechanics of *actually reaching* a million people—social media strategies, video production, hiring team, travel, speaking, producing a book, and all the rest—the conservative estimate was in the millions of dollars. And if, by chance, one of his current videos did go viral and launch his brand, he would *still* need that level of infrastructure in place to keep that momentum going and keep his audience engaged.

"I had no idea," my client told me. "I was resisting the idea that I needed money for this. I just thought, 'If my content is good enough, it will make a difference.' But I also don't want to leave that to chance."

So, let me ask: What does your impact vision *cost*?

- How much does it cost to get your message in front of your tribe?
- How much does it cost to hire the team, the coach, and the other support needed?
- How much does it cost to purchase the equipment, the tech, or the supplies?
- How much does it cost to plant the trees, clean up the rivers, build the schools, or dig the wells?

If you haven't done the math yet, do it now. When you know the numbers, you can set real, measurable goals around them. This process will have a huge impact on your financial vision.

I've already shared with you that I want to feed a billion meals in my lifetime. I also want to plant a billion trees, and cure blindness for a million people. Because I've done the research about how to make this happen and decided which charities I want to work with to accomplish it, I know exactly what my vision will cost.

To be honest, in this exact moment, I don't know exactly what changes in my business will be required to create that $350,000,000 lifetime outcome. But the beauty of this journey is that you don't always need to know the "how." You just have to make a powerful decision, hold the energy of your vision, and keep creating leverage to power them both. When you do this, the Universe will recalibrate around your vision and make the next steps clear, every day. The right people will emerge, the right doors will open, and the right opportunities will present themselves. Trust the process.

I know that if I want to fund my impact vision, I need to move firmly into Circle of Contribution #4. I need to become a wealth circulator. I can't fund my entire impact vision from where I am now ... but a year from now? Five? Ten? Things will look completely different.

Whatever your impact vision is, I want you to know

exactly what it costs, down to the penny. Knowing the numbers will help you build the infrastructure (both visionary and literal) to fully support your MIP.

IT'S THE IMPACT THAT MATTERS

Before we move on, I want to address a big misconception in the impact space: that being "famous" is a prerequisite to impact.

Regardless of what impact space you occupy, visibility will be a part of your business strategy. You *need* to be visible to your ideal clients, donors, or consumers if you want to create real growth and money flow—but there's a difference between being visible *to the right people* and being a celebrity.

Let go of the perception that if you aren't in everyone's inbox, or on everyone's social media feed—if you aren't competing with the Kardashians for screen time—that your impact is somehow lessened. That's absolutely untrue. Not all of us who decide to claim our Maximum Impact Potential will become household names, even if we impact hundreds of millions of humans over the course of our lifetimes. Our ripple effect is not always fully visible, even when we reach the third and fourth Circles of Contribution—and that's okay.

Accolades are nice, but you and I both know that's not why we do what we do. The families benefiting from the food forests I'm planting will never know I was the one to fund their forests. The people whose eyesight is being repaired in developing countries because of my donations will never know my name. It doesn't matter. What matters is that *I* know the impact I'm making—and the knowledge of the change I'm making motivates me to keep going.

THE IMPACT CEO

The most powerful transition I ever made in the impact space was when I moved from being an entrepreneur to being an impact-driven CEO.

Now, you might assume that this shift happened when I took on the title of CEO of Fed by Threads, or even in one of my earlier businesses. You'd be wrong. Just because I *called* myself a CEO didn't mean I knew what it meant to be the Chief Executive Officer of my visionary business.

As an entrepreneur (wearing the CEO shirt), I only wanted to see the upside of my ideas. I didn't want to do things anyone else's way. I didn't want to take advice. I didn't want to look at risk, or ask powerful questions. I just wanted to create my vision my way, and screw everyone else. I had a total Superman complex, and—as I shared in Chapter 4—that led me right off a cliff.

I don't regret any of it, because I would never be where I am today if I hadn't learned those harsh lessons. But you don't have to take the same kind of fall I did in order to start traveling along—as author Keith Cunningham calls it—"The Road Less Stupid."

For those of us who are serial entrepreneurs, our Superman complex evolves out of past successes. Maybe we got really lucky with our first or second businesses, and now we think that because we've done it once, we have the super-secret key that unlocks success in everything. We convince ourselves—and others—that everything we touch will turn to gold.

I scaled multiple businesses to multiple six figures before I was twenty-four years old. (I don't talk about them much these days, but they included a green energy company and some on-campus sales ventures in college.) So, when I came into Fed By Threads, I thought I was sure I was going to crush it.

My fatal mistake was that I hated looking at risk. I didn't even want to entertain the possibility that one of my ideas wouldn't work. I knew my heart was in the right place—but I used that as an excuse not to ask for feedback because I was secretly afraid people would shoot down my ideas and I would be emotionally crushed. My "success strategy" was to put all my chips on the table, cross my fingers, and hope for the best. It had always worked before, so why not now?

The willingness to look at the big picture, assess risk, and make clear decisions based on reality—not wishful thinking—is the difference between a CEO and an entrepreneur. This evolution didn't happen for me as a leader until about a year into my coaching business. But when it did, it triggered a massive expansion of my Maximum Impact Potential. The mature process of logically analyzing, evaluating, and testing each idea has become crucial to my business growth and impact planning. I ask questions like, "Does the market want this idea?" and, "Can my company tolerate this idea not working?"

As impact-driven people, we believe deeply in the goodness of our ideas. We only want to see the upside. We don't want to think that our idea—our heartfelt gift to the world—could possibly be the wrong way to serve our clients and the world. We don't want to consider right timing or market value.

I see this resistance come up at many points in my clients' journeys—but Superman Syndrome kicks in hard when we are looking at their Million Person Impact Plan. Once they know what their vision will actually cost to execute, they want it to be "easy" (and by "easy" I mean "not challenging to their current beliefs, sensibilities, money story, or thought patterns"). They want their *exact ideas* to be the pathway that will get them to the MIP, into the flow of wealth, but they don't want to evaluate those ideas critically or test them in the market before they're launched.

No matter what your actual job title is, you have a choice

about how to show up—as a dreamer, or as a CEO. Dreamers throw spaghetti at the wall, pray for miracles, don't ask for help, and chase short-term gains. They may see big wins—but they also see huge failures which can stunt their MIP for years. Impact-driven CEOs get good advice, ask great questions, assess risk, and make decisions for the long-term. Being that CEO is less exciting, but more satisfying. And when you find that sweet spot where the desire of your heart aligns with the needs of the market, you can move forward in full alignment and grow with unlimited upside.

So, how do you make the shift into CEO-mode?

Three letters. A-S-K.

Certainty is the enemy of possibility. That's why asking for help is the single most powerful tool in any impact-driven leader's toolkit. When you ask, you stop spinning in circles. You tee yourself up. You close the door on dumb mistakes that can cost you years of MIP growth. You become willing to learn as well as lead.

The other key difference between impact entrepreneurs and CEOs is their viewpoint on advancement. When I first opened my coaching business, it was what we call a "personal brand," meaning, *I* was the brand. I was following my vision to create impact within the transformation industry, asking for help constantly, and working daily with what I considered to be a really powerful question: "What new skill does Alok need to add so that he can create more value for his clients, raise his prices, and create more impact flow?"

This was a good premise, but it had one huge flaw: when I reached a point where I was maxed out, my MIP would come to a standstill. Eventually, I would run out of time, bandwidth, or new skills to market. If I added too many unique skills, I would dilute my brand and message. I could actually damage my credibility by trying to integrate too much.

I wondered, *How can I continue to grow without any caps or roadblocks?*

When I conceived my current company brand, Uplifting Millions, I not only shifted away from being a personal brand, I also created a pathway to unlimited upside. Now, instead of asking, "What does Alok need to learn?" I started asking, "What do my clients need in order to create their Maximum Impact Potential and uplift millions?"

From that point, everything changed. My capacity and confidence grew. I was able to hire a killer team with full confidence that they would execute the company mission with the same passion and dedication I bring. I was able to scale my offers without diluting their value.

Unlimited upside—for impact *and* income.

NEVER FORGET YOUR WHY

As I shared in Chapter 2, God didn't bring me my million dollars—at least, not when I was six. But now that I've got the three most important components of impact behind me—decision, vision, and leverage—God has delivered at last, and then some.

Whatever spiritual practices you embrace, I want you to remember one thing. God (or Source, Universe, or whatever you choose to call it) *always* delivers. But in order to align our own energy with the co-creative possibilities available to use *through* God and the Universe, we need to do more than *want*. We need to know *why* we want what we want, and what we intend to do with what we desire when it materializes.

At six years old, my desire was pure. I wanted God to deliver a bunch of money so I could help my family and make people happy. But I didn't include that "why" in my request; I just asked for the cash. If I had been clear on *exactly* what I was going to do with a million bucks and why it mattered, I have no doubt that I would have manifested it effortlessly.

Just take Mikaila Ulmer, founder of Me & The Bees Lemonade. From the age of four, she was fascinated by bees and their contribution to the local ecosystem. At five years old, she decided to start a lemonade stand to benefit organizations fighting to save the bees—and soon ended up on Shark Tank. Ten years later, she is a published author, inspirational speaker, and CEO. She has millions flowing through her organization, and her product is available in

Whole Foods, Kroger, and many other big chain grocery stores—and she's still too young to drive.

Your vision and decision is priceless. When your "why" is bigger than your fears, doubts, or perceived obstacles, you will begin to attract leverage—including money— to your impact dream. It *will* show up. It's inevitable.

I want you to understand that your Million Person Impact Plan isn't just a fun distraction or one of those bullshit busy-work exercises you sometimes see in the coaching space. It is literally the "why" you will deliver to God and the Universe—the deep, clear, vitally important reason why money, resources, and people should flow toward you starting *now*. This clarity allows all of your tactics and strategies to line up around the magic, and creates quantum-level results in record time.

So ... do the work. Get clear on your Million Person Impact Plan—what it is, what it will cost, and how long it will take to implement. Become the impact-driven CEO of your impact space, instead of the entrepreneur, manager, or employee.

Then, ask.

Believe.

And above all, keep showing up at the mailbox.

9 | THE BLUE ZONE EFFECT

IN JULY OF 2021, I went on retreat in Costa Rica with my partner, Caitlin, with a question in my heart: "Where am I going from here?"

My coaching business for impact-driven leaders was exploding. I'd just finished filming my first television show appearance (Season Two of *Four Days to Save the World)*. Caitlin and I had recently moved into our dream home in the hills outside of Tucson, Arizona. I was circulating more wealth in a month than I used to make in a year, and was well on my way to realizing my lifetime vision of planting a billion trees and feeding a billion meals. Life felt magical. I was literally living the dream.

And yet, I knew I still hadn't reached my Maximum Impact Potential. It was like I was nearing the peak of a steep but beautiful mountain, but I still couldn't see what was on the other side. So much of my previous vision had already come into being—but what was next?

When we arrived at Rythmia, the medical resort that would be our home for the week, I learned that we had entered what has become known as a "Blue Zone"—a unique place on Earth that is home to a higher-than-average percentage of people who live to ages greater than 100. There are five such epicenters of longevity on the planet (that we know of): Okinawa, Japan; Sardinia, Italy; Ikaria, Greece; Loma Linda, California; and Nicoya, Costa Rica, where we had just landed. The hallmarks of these locations are not just the long lives of their residents, but nine specific lifestyle habits which *New York Times* best-selling author Dan Buettner chronicled in his best-selling book, *The Blue Zones.*

With the power of a thunderbolt, it landed: the next phase of my journey.

All this time, I'd been following my internal vision toward my Maximum Impact Potential. I'd learned to own my power. I'd become a true wealth circulator. My team and

I—through the vehicle of my company, Uplift Millions—
had created an epicenter of impact in the world of coaching
and sales, and we were expanding that impact every day.

But beyond building my own Impact Empire, what was
I creating?

The answer? A "Blue Zone" *business.*

What if impact-driven businesses could become epicenters of happiness, wealth, and longevity for everyone
who interacted with them?

What if business leaders built companies and made
daily decisions in accordance with established principles
of equity, mental health awareness, environmental responsibility, and wealth circulation?

What if, instead of having only a few tiny "blue zones"
scattered around the planet, we used the vehicle of business to turn the whole world blue?

RED ZONE/BLUE ZONE

Let's face it: most businesses are not Blue Zones. Not for their
employees, not for their customers, and not for our planet.

The last few centuries of modern industry have been
driven by what I'll call "Red Zone" businesses. These are
businesses based on extractionary capitalism, where
everything is expendable in the relentless pursuit of profit.
Workers are expendable. Life is expendable. Nature is

expendable. This way of operating serves and prioritizes the few (usually white men) at the top, while excluding everyone else. It's the backward-flowing infinity loop we discussed in Chapter 6.

Now, we're at a pivot point. More than 85 percent of the original Fortune 500 companies are gone. Not just off the list. *Gone.* The average length of time that a business spends on the S&P 500 has shrunk by 36 percent. This is a huge shift in the landscape. But who will step in to fill the shoes (and the market shares) of those Red Zone giants?

As impact-driven leaders, our job is to look into the future. In a landscape where change is accelerating faster than ever before in history, would you really bet on the old model as a path to success? Even as I write this, leading companies like Google and Microsoft are pushing toward new ideals like carbon neutrality and wage equality. Wall Street is having a hard time convincing bankers that working seventy-hour weeks is the only way to get those big bonuses. Millennials in particular have shown that they want to work for companies whose missions align with their own—even if it means taking a significant pay cut.

The pandemic of 2020 has only accelerated this shift. As I write this, the business world is preparing for what's being called "The Great Resignation." People have seen that the Red Zone way isn't the only way—and they're determined not to go back to the way things were.

Maximum Impact Potential is about realizing your personal impact in the world through your work and daily decisions. When you own your value, become a wealth circulator, and create your Million Person Impact Plan, you will become an even greater force for good in the world.

And, when you begin living your MIP, the Red Zone model of extractionary capitalism will become anathema to you. Once you've seen the truth, you can't turn back.

A Blue Zone business is the natural creation of a leader who is truly living their MIP. It's a wealth-circulating ecosystem that operates on a system of non-negotiable values and aims to perpetuate the health, vitality, happiness, and impact of everyone who works with and within it. It doesn't matter if the business itself is a massive coaching platform, a tech startup, or a small-town pizza restaurant—the principles are exactly the same. Being in the Blue Zone is about being part of an integrated whole and leading from impact.

And what makes a business a Blue Zone business? It starts with a Blue Zone Leader.

BLUE ZONE LEADERSHIP

Exploring your MIP is only one piece of becoming a Blue Zone Leader. The other is excavating your inner bullshit.

Yes. I said it.

We all have stories. We all have trauma. We all have fears. And those inner experiences shape how we lead in our lives and businesses—whether we know it or not.

Red Zone businesses are overwhelmingly helmed by men who have, quite frankly, shut off their feelings. In corporate culture (and in our Western culture in general), it's considered weak to show emotion. Excitement? Sure. But compassion? Empathy? Sadness? Uncertainty? Those are to be avoided at all costs.

But something happens to humans when we consistently jam our natural expression down like trash in a trash compactor. We harden. Grow rigid. Forget how to connect.

Red Zone companies—the ones driven by profit at all costs—require emotionless leadership. Weakness is to be destroyed. Obstacles are to be obliterated. Workers are liabilities, not assets. Women and people of color are not to be coddled with things like equal pay or maternity leave. This cold, calculating mentality is the founding principle of Red Zone Businesses, and while it might serve the shareholders and a few people at the top quite well, it's the worst possible sort of leadership for the collective and our planet. How many times have you witnessed someone make an unethical decision and then say with a shrug, "That's just business."

Blue Zone Leaders want to lead differently. They know that impact starts with them committing to their own MIP, but it doesn't stop there.

Rather than make coldly logical decisions from some arbitrary "bottom line," they are ready to see their businesses as entities in flow within an interconnected whole.

Rather than tolerate gender inequality and pay gaps, they are committed to rooting out internal biases (even in themselves) to level the playing field.

Rather than sacrifice the environment for short-term gain, they take internal measures to align their supply chains, products, and services with real sustainability.

Rather than label mental health as a "woo-woo" focus, they focus on emotional well-being for their teams. They heal their own traumas around masculine energy, misogyny, and societal programming so those traumas don't play out in their leadership.

Rather than pay the bare minimum salary for each position, they commit to paying their teams a living wage.

Rather than making charity and volunteer work something that employees do on their own time, they build it into the company culture.

When we become Blue Zone Leaders, we tap into the ultimate expression of our MIP. We become part of a new generation of leadership. And when we do it together, in community with other Blue Zone Leaders, we can also create the support we need to stay the course, even when it's tempting to go back into the Red Zone.

At the time of this writing, I'm still formulating the

nuances of Blue Zone Leadership and what it will look like in practice—but I know on a soul-deep level that bringing this concept to the world is the next step in realizing my own Maximum Impact Potential. Perhaps it will be part of your MIP, too.

YOUR FIRST STEPS INTO THE BLUE ZONE

If what I've shared in this chapter resonates with you, chances are you've been considering what it would mean to make your business a Blue Zone Business (even though you didn't use that term). What would it mean for your business to be as much of a force for change as you, yourself, have become?

Like Adam Goodman, whose story I shared in Chapter 4, you may decide to make a powerful pivot when you connect to and begin to express your Maximum Impact Potential. My advice is: pick the thing that matters most to you, and start there. Whether that's auditing your payroll to spot any unrecognized wage gaps, tweaking your supply chain to include more environmentally-friendly vendors, re-imagining your base pay structure to ensure that everyone makes a living wage, or something else entirely, remember that small changes now will add up to big impact later.

10 | LIVING IMPACT

MY SON SEQUOIA still talks about the day we bought a homeless man a pizza.

We were heading to Time Market in Tucson for a slice of his favorite pie when we saw a man sitting on the side of the road. It was obvious that he was struggling. As we parked and made our way to the door, I said, "Hey kiddo, how do you feel about buying that man a pizza?"

"Okay," Sequoia said. "That would be good, I guess."

We bought our own dinner, plus a big slice for the dude outside. But when we got back to the parking lot, he was nowhere to be found.

Up and down the streets we drove, peering into every alley and doorway. About thirty minutes later, we found the guy on a side street—totally unaware, of course, that we'd been searching for him with the intensity of federal investigators on a manhunt.

"Why don't you give him the pizza," I suggested to my son. So he did. He marched up, no-longer-steaming box in hand, and introduced himself while the man watched him warily. Then, the puzzled look gave way to a smile, and he shook Sequoia's hand and introduced himself. "I'm Charles," he said. "It's nice to meet you."

Back in the car, Sequoia was quiet for a while. Then, he met my eyes in the rear view mirror, and said, "Dad, I like that we give food to people who are hungry."

We never saw Charles again after that day. I sometimes wonder what happened to him—but in the end, that's not really what this story is about. Feeding someone you meet on the street is a small thing—but the *impact consciousness* of "we give food to people who are hungry" is profound. That experience was probably even more meaningful for my son than it was for Charles. Years later, he still remembers it. I hope he never forgets.

Now that Sequoia is older, we're having more conversations about impact. We just moved into a beautiful new home in the mountains outside of Tucson—a far cry from the one-room studio I was living in just five short years ago. Sequoia is super excited to show the place off to his friends—an excitement that can quickly slide sideways into entitlement. We talk often about the idea of being wealth circulators, and how the money flowing through our family isn't just for us, but for everyone around us, too. My hope is that he sees beyond what's in it for him, and embraces the big picture of our impact as a family—our vision, our values, and our legacy.

When you embrace the lessons you've learned in this book and start to put them to work in your life and business, you will step into a space that I call "living impact." Thinking like an Impact CEO, working strategically to expand into your next Circle of Contribution, moving through your mission and becoming a wealth circulator ... the very act of doing these things will change you at a core level. You will literally become a force for change no matter what space you occupy. Whether it's something as big as changing the nature of global currency, or something as small as buying a random dude a pizza, you will leave a path of change wherever you go.

A GLOBAL PICTURE

Maybe you've heard this analogy about strength in numbers: One pencil is easy to break. But put ten in your hand, and there's no way you can splinter them. Put a hundred pencils together, and you can hold up a house. (Maybe no one has ever actually tried that last experiment, but you get the picture.) The power of a mission becomes exponentially stronger the more people are working together to create it.

You will absolutely experience this dynamic as you grow your impact business and build your team. But you will also experience it in other ways—most profoundly when you witness other people doing their own impact work in spaces and communities that overlap your own.

As we discussed in Chapter 8, the amazing thing about building an impact empire is that we can share our Human Geographic Footprint with other empire builders. Together, we build a multi-layered web of support, inspiration, and impact for individuals, communities, and the planet. We add more pencils to the stack, and the whole stack becomes stronger.

Your expression of your Maximum Impact Potential isn't limited to the work you do in your business, or even what you do within your family. When you embrace the idea of your HGF and stop buying into the old mindsets of competition and scarcity, you will begin to see opportunities to leverage other people's impact empires to maximize your own contribution. Talk about a win-win! Soon, instead of a bunch of niche giants staking their claim to an impact space, we have an army of impact-driven, global thinkers who are working together to facilitate change.

Van Jones, the CNN anchor, recently used the term "Love Army" in this context. He wasn't speaking about the 1960s "peace, pot, and protests" vibe, but rather about a core group of people who are focusing concerted effort into actions and projects that will create global outcomes on a grand scale. A veritable army of movers and shakers who see the world as a beautiful place in the process of becoming more beautiful.

For perhaps the first time in human history, our collective energy is shifting away from self-preservation and survivalism to collective expansion and evolution. When you embrace the path to your Maximum Impact Potential, you become a member of that Love Army—a force for good in this world that strengthens the web already being woven, and adds a new dimension of support for others who are ready to embrace their full potential.

We're beginning to see (in America, at least) a growing body of evidence that wealth and impact consciousness is changing at a generational level. There's an intergenerational transfer of ideas afoot, and the younger population is beginning to normalize some of the stuff that was a tough sell to previous generations—like valuing experiences over material goods, practicing real diversity and inclusion, and choosing a work path based on impact rather than income. For example, Millennials are more and more choosing to work for companies whose missions and values align with their own, even when it means taking a pay cut. When you think about an entire generation collectively valuing their MIP more than their wallets ... the possibilities are staggering. It's just one expression of the long-term ripple we're creating as conscious entrepreneurs and intrapreneurs. This isn't some pipe dream that might materialize four generations down the line. We're already seeing the shift.

Despite these exciting developments, however, we still have a lot of work to do. The vast majority of the world is still laboring in the old paradigm. They see themselves as cogs in a wheel, powerless to change anything, needing to game the system to get ahead (or even just survive the month). It's our job as impact-driven movement makers to keep braving the heat of the spotlight to create a groundswell that can lift *all* of humanity into a new normal.

MIP, UNLEASHED

It's my hope that, whatever your beliefs were before you picked up this book, you are closing the cover unable to go back to your old ways of being. That what you've learned has unleashed a fire within you that will fuel you to step more fully into your Maximum Impact Potential than ever before. That you are asking new questions about what you are capable of, and how you will be remembered. That together, we have opened the door to creating a better world for all current and future generations.

You and I are the crazy ones. We believe, deep in our core, that we can make a difference. And even though we all have jaded moments where we think otherwise, I hope that this book has re-anchored you into the truth that you are no more or less capable than anyone else, and that *you were born to do this work.*

Remember that reaching your Maximum Impact Potential is a marathon, not a sprint. You don't need to save the world overnight. Just find that first domino and knock it over. Then, find the next one ... and keep going. A mere few years from now, you will be able to gaze back and soak up the magic of a life lived to its fullest potential.

Above all, remember that you matter. Your voice matters. Your mission matters. And you always have within you the power to uplift millions.

You're only ever one decision away.

AFTERWORD

WHEN I WAS TEACHING in New York, I met a for-
ty-year veteran teacher named Maggie DeLuca. Maggie was
a tough old bird, but she loved her students deeply. As the
leader of an urban education initiative in New York's public
schools, she dealt with some of the most challenging situa-
tions in the teaching world.

"Alok," she once said to me. "We will never fully know
the long-term impact that we make. We just won't. We can't.

We are the invisible hand."

Sometimes, people will come back to us and share how we've changed their lives. But most of the time, they won't. That doesn't mean our work was without value. We—all of us—are invisible hands, guiding the expansion and upliftment of others in our world.

After reading this book, you understand fully how to tap into the powers of decision, vision, and leverage to reach your Maximum Impact Potential. I have no doubt that you will positively impact millions of lives through your work, and if this book gave legs to even a tiny fraction of that impact, I am grateful. Thank you for allowing me to become part of your Human Geographic Footprint—and for becoming part of mine.

When you put your ideas out in the world—when you topple that first domino—you become responsible for the impact you are creating, even if you can't see it. And while it's nice when the world applauds you for your effort, there's joy to be found regardless. You can choose to feel and embrace the impact that you're creating even if it may rarely be mirrored back to you directly.

Several years ago, my father co-founded PUKAR, the Partners for Urban Knowledge Action & Research initiative. It evolved from a simple idea: instead of giving a person a fish, or even giving him a fishing rod, teach him to research how to make his own fishing equipment.

PUKAR empowers the urban poor to become researchers of their own situation. Rather than sending Harvard-trained researchers into the slums of India to make their own assertions about what people need—in essence, swooping in to "save" the poor of Mumbai from their current reality—PUKAR invites members of the community to gather information from the vantage point of their lived experience and leverage it to create meaningful change. It's the epitome of "the invisible hand."

What a singular idea my father birthed. When we empower people to be powerful creators of their own lives, rather than victims of their circumstances, we water that seed of greatness within them.

As you move into the fullest expression of your own MIP, armed with the knowledge in this book and your own accumulated wisdom and experience, I want you to remember that you are Gandhi. I am Gandhi. And every one of the people you are seeking to serve are Gandhi. All of us—regardless of where we are in life right now—are born with the same capacity and potential for impact.

As you continue to multiply the weight and height of your dominoes, get money moving through your mission, and build your impact empire, it can be tempting to forget that basic truth. It's gratifying when people praise you. It's nice when you get to "save the day." But in the end, the world will be best served if we all think like our most beloved teachers—if we see ourselves as the "invisible hand," and do our best for everyone who crosses our path, even if we never know whether or not we made a difference.

RESOURCES

JOIN THE UPLIFT MILLIONS NETWORK!

A community and training platform for coaches, consultants, experts, and leaders who want to monetize their knowledge, touch more lives, and change the world.

WE.UPLIFTMILLIONS.COM

LEARN MORE ABOUT OUR WORK

Book a discovery call with the Uplift Millions team to learn more about how we can support you to build your 6- or 7-figure impact business, crack the money code, and touch more lives.

UPLIFTMILLIONS.COM/MAX

BOOK ALOK TO SPEAK

Email alok@upliftmillions.com with your request. Please include event information, date(s), and requested topics.

ACKNOWLEDGMENTS

I NEED TO GIVE a shout out to so many people who have supported me throughout my life and believed in me, including: my family in Upstate NY, my family in India, the West Philly gang, my friends from Francis Parker High School, and the crew from Wesleyan University.

I'd also love to thank the following backers who contributed to this project: Dee Frame Hourigan, Penny Cole, Eric Clarke, Briana Crane, Brooke McDonald, Amber Bieg,

Lindsay L. Mikus, Sara Breckenridge, Rachel Levin Albert, Leah Vidal, Pia Ruokis, Aurora Breckenfeld, Kristine Scher, Sally Weber, Kylie Rogers, Lauren, Heidi Hadley, Quinlan Wilhite, Bruce Bowditch, Vicki Willan, Stacey Druss, Deborah Genovesi, Nancy Fasino, Jen Hermesmeyer, Bonnie M. Goble, Ray Hills, Serena Gabriel, Nilaya Sabnis, Carol Fisher, Delbert G. Sutton Jr., and Kathryn Reynolds. Thank you for helping me bring this book to life at long last.

ABOUT THE AUTHOR

ALOK APPADURAI was born in Philadelphia, PA in 1978 and has dedicated his life to making a positive impact in the world. He's launched four impact-driven companies, three in the industries of clean energy, global media for women, and sustainable clothing, as well as his most recent company, Uplift Millions, a coaching company for entrepreneurs who value people, planet, and profit.

He graduated from Wesleyan University in 2000 where

he built his own major combining Economics, History & Literature and then went on to teach third through sixth grades in New York City before launching his career in social entrepreneurship.

In 2015, Alok gave a TEDx Talk on feeding hundreds of thousands of emergency meals to people in need. He was nominated for the Gifted Citizen award, has been recognized by the Ashoka Foundation's "Threads For Thought" competition, and has been a speaker for multiple social entrepreneurship summits and events.

Much of Alok's professional career has been spent creating businesses that uplift women, in particular. He believes the world gets better when more money flows through more women.

Alok's travels to more than thirty countries on five continents (including visits to the Mother Teresa House in Calcutta and the slums of Johannesburg), combined with growing up in West Philadelphia, have shaped his dedication to making other peoples' lives better, but the most transformative day of his life thus far was the day his son, Sequoia, was born.

Alok wears his heart on his sleeve, enjoys making hand-poured candles, and loves to ski. His favorite food is masala dosa, and whenever he eats Ben & Jerry's ice cream, he thinks of his late mother, Carol.

ABOUT THE PUBLISHER

FOUNDED IN 2021 by Bryna Haynes, WorldChangers Media is a boutique publishing company focused on "Ideas for Impact." We know that great books change lives, topple outdated paradigms, and build movements. Our commitment is to deliver superior-quality transformational nonfiction by, and for, the next generation of thought leaders.

Ready to write and publish your thought leadership book with us? Learn more at www.WorldChangers.Media.

CPSIA information can be obtained
at www.ICGtesting.com
Printed in the USA
BVHW030850130122
626143BV00016B/171/J

9 780999 399163